The Everyday Vegan

The *Everyday* Vegan

RECIPES & LESSONS FOR LIVING THE VEGAN LIFE

Dreena Burton

ARSENAL PULP PRESS

VANCOUVER

ARSENAL PULP PRESS
103-1014 Homer Street
Vancouver, B.C.
Canada V6B 2W9
www.arsenalpulp.com

The publisher gratefully acknowledges the support of the Government of Canada through the
Book Publishing Industry Development Program for its publishing activities.

Book design by Lisa Eng-Lodge
Production assistant Judy Yeung
Food photography and cover photograph by Greg Athans
Food styling by Nathan Fong
Author photograph by Rob Krochenski
Printed and bound in Canada

CANADIAN CATALOGUING IN PUBLICATION DATA:
Burton, Dreena, 1970-
  The everyday vegan

  Includes index.
  ISBN 1-55152-106-7

  1. Vegan cookery.   2. Veganism.   I. Title.
TX837.B87 2001   641.5'636   C2001-911289-0

Table of Contents

Dedication

To my husband, Paul, for your extraordinary support, loyalty, and love.

Acknowledgments

Deepest love and gratitude to my husband Paul: you are unconditionally loving and supportive in everything we do; I could not ask for more in a husband and best friend. I am truly blessed to be part of your "team," and give thanks for you and our precious daughter each day. To my lovable cats Sarabi and Mookie, for all the companionship and "lap warmth" provided over the years.

To my mother and father who gave so much to ensure that opportunities would always be available for my sisters and me: Mom, you are a remarkable woman, loved and respected by so many for the kindness and generosity you continually show as a mother and friend.

To Al and Doreen Smith: your dedication to lifestyle change during trying times inspired me to share my knowledge further. Your commitment is appreciated by all who can benefit from many more years of your love – and your renewed enthusiasm for life!

To my friends and family who supported this book and appreciated my vegan meals: special thanks to my dear friend Tanya Wilkshire; I greatly appreciated the feedback you offered through testing and sharing my recipes. Thank you as well for your incredible enthusiasm for my cooking, and for your acceptance of vegan eating (including tofu!). To my sister Diane, for all of the great vegan meals we shared at her home, but mostly for the ones she delivered to us after our baby was born. To her husband Bill, for sharing his knowledge of the publishing industry with me. To Evan Roche, who contributed his creativity to develop some fun names for my recipes such as "Swallow-It-All Banana Balls!" To our friends, Brian and Amanda Eydt, for the brainstorming fun; Brian, I am glad to have you as my financial advisor (rather than my marketing consultant – "where's the meat" – sorry, you know I can't resist poking fun!). To my former business colleague, Trevor Adey, for the professional development I experienced working with you for three years. The confidence and maturity I gained has been invaluable to this project, as well as others I will work on in the future.

To the skilled professionals who helped to bring this book to life: Li Eng-Lodge for design work; Greg Athans for food photography; Nathan Fong for food styling; and Rob Krochenski for my personal photo on the back cover.

To the organizations and individuals who assisted with the primary research for my book, including Gary and Naty King, EarthSave Canada, the International Vegetarian Union (IVU), and Dave Smith, as well as all of the respondents to my survey. Thanks also to Sterling Haglund for your hard work to repair my computer, which crashed at a less than convenient moment; to Paul Knowles for your time and insight, which was of great help; and to Marilyn Thiessen and Carolyn Downey for introducing us.

To all of the individuals and groups, who choose the healthy and compassionate vegan lifestyle, and support activities towards its increased presence and growth in society. Special thanks to Ingrid Newkirk, one of the most gentle and caring people I have had the pleasure of meeting.

Of course none of this would be possible without the vision and co-operation of everyone at Arsenal Pulp Press, especially Brian Lam.

Introduction

WHO IS *THE EVERYDAY VEGAN*?

There are two ways to interpret the title of this book. In one way, *The Everyday Vegan* is for committed vegans looking for ideas, recipes, and instructions they can use *every day* of the year. In another, the book is for average (i.e., *everyday*) people who want to start eating healthy but don't know where or how to begin. In fact, *The Everyday Vegan* is a great resource for both.

Obviously, I would love to see everyone adopt this healthy diet every day of the year. Our environment would be cleaner, our bodies healthier, and our animals happier. However, I realize that not everyone will change their eating habits overnight. I also know that it is better for people to embrace this delicious, nutritious way of eating occasionally rather than not at all. So use this book if you want to enjoy cooking and eating delicious vegan foods, whether it is every day or any day.

There is no mystery to vegan cooking. If you have been previously stalled by start-up questions – What ingredients do I use? What exactly are they? Where do I get them? What do I do with them once I get them? How do they taste? – you will find the answers here. I frequently use a number of ingredients that may be new to you, but there is an entire section detailing what these ingredients are and where you can find them. There is also a "tips and how-to's" section to help you with cooking techniques and ingredients you may be unfamiliar with. And within the individual recipes, sidebar notes outline substitution ideas, serving suggestions, and other general tips.

The recipe directions are fairly lengthy and detailed, but this does not mean they are complicated; in fact, most are quite easy to prepare. I simply wanted to provide you with instructions clear enough for any cooking level. As an amateur chef, I have learned from cookbooks, cooking shows, literature, and plain experimentation, which proves that anyone can make these recipes!

As for taste, these creations are truly delicious. Vegan food can taste fabulous! Many people who have tried a vegan recipe that is bland or otherwise unappealing think every vegan meal must be the same; this is simply not true. A little experimentation and an open mind are all that is needed to see how scrumptious vegan foods can be! As an example, some soymilks taste awful, but others are excellent. And salads can be wonderful, but vegans can't survive on lettuce alone. The meals I cook have great variety and substance, and friends are often surprised when they eat with us. You too will be surprised when you use these recipes.

An important note about my recipes: you obviously will not find butter as an ingredient, but you also won't find margarine or other hydrogenated oils. Many vegan cookbooks use margarine to replace butter in dishes, particularly for baking and desserts. I eliminated margarine from my diet several years ago, along with other products containing hydrogenated and partially hydrogenated oils. While there are non-hydrogenated margarines available, you will see that I have simplified my cooking by using oils such as olive and canola.

I know from experience that opting for a vegan lifestyle opens you to criticism from others, a situation which can often prove challenging. Common questions include "Where do you get your protein?" and "Aren't you worried about getting osteoporosis?" To address these issues, I have referenced many statistics in the section entitled "No Need for Everyday Concerns," which demonstrate that protein and calcium deficiencies, among other things, are nothing more than myths associated with the vegan diet. In fact, this section reveals that a vegan diet can actually protect against some of our most common and severe ailments and illnesses.

I hope you enjoy using this book. If you would like to share your story, or if you have questions or suggestions for recipe ideas that you would like to see in the future, you can join *The Everyday Vegan* community at: www.everydayvegan.com

Stories of Everyday Vegans
My Family's Story

I grew up in a traditional meat and potatoes family, the fifth of six daughters. Except for a few too many trips to the corner store to sneak junk food, I ate the standard North American diet until I was about seventeen, when I significantly cut back on beef after reading an article about how our bodies digest red meat. I continued to eat just about everything else, including chicken, pork, fish, cheese, and milk; in fact, these were the main ingredients of almost every meal I cooked after I left home to attend university.

I got married at the age of twenty-three, about six months after graduating from university with a business degree. I continued to cook the same dairy-rich, meat-based meals that we had been accustomed to eating, with the exception of red meat. My husband Paul laughed at my red meat theory and even though we didn't eat it at home, he routinely ordered steak or hamburgers when we ate out at restaurants. This continued for about a year, when I took an interest in some literature on vegetarian food I had stumbled across. After more research into the vegetarian lifestyle, I came to the realization that making this kind of dietary change was a very logical step; I was particularly struck by the similarities between our digestive systems and those of herbivores in the wild. Thus I began to experiment with vegetarian foods.

Our subsequent transition to a vegan diet does not make for great storytelling. There was no true defining moment or major revelation, no cleaning out of cupboards or memorable final meat-based meal. In fact, our switch was quite gradual, if not downright slow. I first switched to eating free-range chicken and eggs, but soon realized that the proper thing to do was to stop consuming poultry products altogether. I don't believe I ever saw free-range pork products and if memory serves me correctly I decided to eliminate pork, fish, and all other animal flesh from my diet at the same time I stopped eating poultry. Officially I could call myself a vegetarian, but not a vegan.

Paul sort of fell into these changes, since I was doing all of the cooking. While he didn't initiate the transition, he didn't miss meat either, and after a month or so of vegetarian meals he stopped ordering meat in restaurants. Somewhere along the way, his palate came to appreciate the great flavors that vegan meals offer. He now laughs when people ask him, "Don't you sometimes crave a nice juicy steak?" The fact is that he finds the very thought of eating meat unappealing to the point that he has difficulty even watching others eat it, or seeing it prepared on television cooking shows.

Eliminating dairy products was more difficult for us. Like most people, we had accepted all of the media messages received since birth and firmly believed that our bodies needed milk. I don't think it helped that our local grocer had a limited selection of soymilks and other milk product substitutes that didn't taste very good. So we continued consuming dairy for about a year as I read and learned more, keeping an open mind about the information available on dairy products, and the source of that information. Soon, I came to the understanding that cow's milk is meant for baby cows just as a human mother's milk is meant for baby humans! After all, no one would ever venture out into a pasture and nurse directly from a cow. So why consume cow's milk when other animals do not drink milk from other species, or drink it from their own once weaned?

As a result, we decided to begin eliminating dairy from our diet. The results had such a remarkable impact that we have not consumed dairy products since. My digestion improved remarkably and I noticed that I contracted fewer head colds and flues than I had in the past – not that I never get colds anymore, but I get significantly fewer, and they are much shorter in duration. My knees improved, too. I recall having such stiffness and pain in my knees that once during a university presentation, it was painful to stand up from my chair. At the time, all I could think was "I am twenty, and my knees feel horrible; what will they be like when I am forty or fifty?" I was consuming a lot of dairy at that time – yogurt, frozen yogurt, cheese, and milk. The removal of dairy products, I believe, was key to the improvements in my knees and the elimination of other health concerns that were unusual for such a young age.

Paul also felt better. At least once a year, before becoming vegan, Paul contracted a serious throat infection which required antibiotics. At one point he was scheduled to have his tonsils removed, but didn't because of an unexpected trip out of town. He did not reschedule his appointment and in the past six years since becoming vegan, his annual throat infections have disappeared and he has not been on antibiotics once. He firmly believes his vegan diet is the difference.

These changes were the turning point in our transition to a vegan diet. The proof was in our physical health and feeling of well-being. Now, the more we continue to read and learn, the more literature and research supports our personal truths.

So why this book? When we first started eating vegan, I was often disappointed in the recipes I tried. They often lacked the full flavor and textures I was looking for, and many required a lot of new ingredients that were sometimes costly, difficult to find, and infrequently used. I enjoyed experimenting on my own, and soon found a passion in vegan cooking. Over the years, I learned about new cooking techniques and different foods that expanded my recipe creations. Friends and family frequently asked for my recipes, as well as for food and cooking information, and they often told me that I should be working professionally in this field, an idea that was appealing to me. When Paul's parents decided to change their diet too (see: "Al & Doreen's Story" which follows), I realized the value of my recipes and food knowledge. Inspired by their remarkable success and commitment, I left a corporate career to write this book.

As I was finishing the manuscript, I gave birth to our first child. A vegan from the day she was conceived, our daughter is a happy, healthy bundle of joy who will grow and be nourished by the great foods you will find in this book.

Al & Doreen's Story

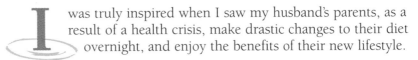

I was truly inspired when I saw my husband's parents, as a result of a health crisis, make drastic changes to their diet overnight, and enjoy the benefits of their new lifestyle.

In 1998, at the age of sixty-one, Paul's father, Al, experienced a heart attack. It was a huge shock to anyone who knew him, as he didn't fit the stereotype for someone at risk for heart disease. He wasn't overweight, he didn't smoke or drink, and his diet was not bad by North American standards. He didn't eat a lot of junk food or take-out, but he did consume animal products regularly.

At the time of his heart attack, Paul and I had been vegan for about five years, but we didn't impose our lifestyle on others, especially family. It was therefore somewhat of a surprise when Paul's mother, Doreen, approached me that first night in the hospital and announced that they wanted to switch to a vegan diet.

Apparently, Al explicitly told his cardiologist that he wanted to make changes so that this would never happen again and he could return to a healthy, happy life. His cardiologist, who coincidentally was a vegetarian, said that if he really wanted to improve his health, a dietary change was absolutely necessary. Other lifestyle changes were also required, including more exercise and taking steps to reduce stress. Although Al had an angioplasty procedure, his cardiologist explained that this procedure alone would not prevent future heart attacks nor reverse his heart disease. It was simply the immediate first step required for Al to begin his recovery.

The cardiologist recommended a book entitled *Dr. Dean Ornish's Program for Reversing Heart Disease*. This reversal diet excludes all animal products except egg whites and non-fat dairy products, with very limited fat intake, and advocates other lifestyle changes, including regular exercise. Al chose to exclude all animal products from his diet, including dairy and eggs, but ate fish just occasionally.

Paul and I were thrilled to provide the practical help that got them started with their transition. While Al was recovering in the hospital, I prepared meals for both of them using some of my recipes, and Paul delivered them every night. It gave them a chance to see how tasty this healthful food can be. They didn't have to worry that their new diet would be uninteresting! Within the first few days, Doreen cleared all animal products out of her cupboards and fridge, and began asking what foods could be used to replace some of their staples (for example, soy milk instead of cow's milk). She went shopping right away, picking up many of the items we suggested. As they started cooking and experimenting, I answered questions along the way. Before long, they impressed us with their own creations! As part of their new lifestyle, they also began walking an hour every day, and found more time to relax and enjoy the little things in life.

That was a full three years ago. With each physical, Al's cardiologist has noted improvements in his condition. But his medical check-ups are not the only measure of their newfound improved health. Al has lost twenty pounds, and Doreen has lost twenty-five. Also, prior to their lifestyle change, results from a bone density test indicated that Doreen was at risk for developing osteoporosis, but two years later, the same test has shown bone density improvements! And her asthma has improved to the point that she no longer uses an inhaler. They rarely get colds or flues anymore, even though they used to get at least one or two a year. And they were both very flattered at a ten-year office reunion when former colleagues expressed amazement at how young and fit they both looked. Al's most recent check-up was impresssive: his cardiologist stated that Al is one of only a very few patients who have been able to keep their cholesterol under control with diet and exercise.

Al and Doreen's commitment is admirable. First, they made this switch later in life, when most people are resistant or indifferent to change. Secondly, they continue to eat vegan in a city where vegetarian options in restaurants are very limited, and there are just a couple of health food stores. They often make special requests at grocery and health food stores to carry the products they want. On a recent cross country trip to Florida, Doreen made meals and snacks along the way so they could eat healthy during their week of travel without having to worry about what vegan options the roadside diners may or may not have. These ongoing examples of their dedication and success make me think, "If they can be everyday vegans, anyone can"!

Tanya's Story

Tanya Wilkshire, one of my best friends, is a vibrant and healthy mother of two adorable kids, Matthew, five, and Kate, two. Healthy eating and lifestyle choices had always interested her, and she was somewhat curious about our vegan diet. She occasionally expressed interest in preparing vegan meals, but for as long as I had known her she had a major aversion to tofu. The very thought of it – its look, its feel – made her feel ill.

One of my funniest "Tanya tofu" memories occurred about five years ago when she and her husband Nick were at our house for a dessert night. I had made a chocolate pudding pie using soft dessert-style tofu. I served it to Nick and Tanya, and they appeared to be enjoying it. Nick was ready for seconds, and Tanya was happily finishing her first piece until she asked what was in it. The minute I said "tofu," she immediately put down her fork and stopped eating. Poor Nick felt guilty as he sheepishly helped himself to another piece, but Tanya could not get past the mental block of eating tofu, even though she appeared to love the taste and texture before she knew what it was.

So it was a major breakthrough when they stayed at our home last year for a visit (we now live in different cities) and Tanya said she was ready to try a meal with tofu in it. She explained that she would be fine as long as she couldn't see the tofu in its regular form. The finished product had to somehow disguise the tofu – no big chunks of the white stuff to bite through. I thought my "Sweet and Sour Neat Balls" would be perfect. In this recipe, I first purée firm or extra-firm tofu in a food processor until it is powdery fine, then mix it with the ingredients to form the "Neat Balls," served with a sweet and sour sauce. I did a quick demo for Tanya while preparing the meal, so she could see how I worked with the tofu.

"They're actually quite good," she noted pleasantly after her first bite. I was happy to have partially broken through her tofu barrier. The next day, she was open to a few more options.

I gave Tanya some recipes and cooking tips to take home, specifically asking her to keep them to herself until my book was published. She began experimenting at home, trying new foods. In just a few weeks, she was including more vegan meals in her diet, which her whole family enjoyed. Five-year-old Matthew particularly likes the "Chickpea Mash Stew."

Tanya also made some vegan meals for guests, and had friends try leftovers when they visited. Some asked for the recipes, but Tanya told them that she couldn't give them out until my book was published. This apparently caused some upset, to the point that Tanya decided she wouldn't make any more of my recipes for guests until the book was out. I enjoyed this compliment, of course, but what really made me happy was that Tanya and her family were appreciating the tastes and health benefits of vegan foods.

Tanya now enjoys tofu many different ways, experimenting with recipes and the vegan diet in general. She and her family recently removed dairy from their diets, and have been "dairy-free" for the past few months. Although Tanya initially thought that she could never exclude milk and other dairy from her family's diet, she has already decided that they will no longer consume dairy.

Tanya, Nick, Matthew, and Kate are a great example of an "everyday vegan" family. They experimented with vegan foods, gradually including more their daily meals. Knowing how delicious and rewarding vegan eating can be, it has now become part of their healthy lifestyle.

Shopping for Everyday Ingredients
What They Are, Where to Get Them, How to Use Them

Here is some information on some of the recipe ingredients I use that may be new to you, as well as where to shop for them and how to use them. Some of the items may also be used as substitution ideas or to jazz up recipes in general. In this section you will find:

FRESH HERBS
Basil
Chives
Cilantro/Coriander
Dill
Oregano
Parsley
Rosemary
Tarragon
Thyme

GRAINS & FLOURS
Arborio Rice
Arrowroot Flour
Chickpea Flour
Couscous
Kamut Flour
Millet
Phyllo Pastry
Quinoa
Wild Rice
Whole Wheat Pastry Flour

NUTS & SEEDS
Almond Butter
Flax Seeds/Flax Meal
Tahini

SOY PRODUCTS
Miso
Soy Milk
Soy/Rice Cheeses
Tamari
Tofu

SPICES SEASONING & CONDIMENTS
Egg-Free, Non-Dairy
   Mayonnaise
Balsamic Vinegar
Chipotle Hot Sauce
Fenugreek
Hoisin Sauce
Lemongrass
Red Wine Vinegar
Rice Vinegar
Sea Salt
Vanilla Bean

SWEETENERS & CHOCOLATE
Blackstrap Molasses
Honey Options
Chocolate and
   Chocolate Chips
Stevia
Unrefined Sugar

Fresh Herbs

Fresh herbs are easily grown at home in the garden or on a window sill, but they are also readily available in the produce section of most grocery stores. Selection will vary at times, and generally herbs other than parsley and cilantro are packed in small plastic containers. Parsley and cilantro are usually kept with the other produce items, left open in large bunches.

BASIL: Basil is one of my favorite herbs. It is wonderfully aromatic, but it is one of the more perishable and delicate herbs. It can bruise (blacken) easily and needs to be treated with a little TLC. To use the leaves, simply tear them away from the stalk. In order to minimize bruising, use a very sharp knife to chop the leaves, or tear them with your hands. The taste of dried basil does not compare with fresh, so is not always a good substitute. Generally, dried basil works well in dishes such as soups and stocks, where it can be added early in the cooking process and will contribute to the overall flavor. Basil works wonderfully with tomato-based dishes, bell peppers, many pastas, and Italian dishes, to name just a few.

CHIVES: Chives are part of the onion family and can be used in many dishes. They can be easily chopped and added to salads, used in dips and dressings, or to garnish various entrées. They work well with many different foods, with potatoes at the top of the list. Scallions, or green onions, can be substituted for chives, but only use the top tender green portions, chopped fine, since they are somewhat stronger than chives.

CILANTRO/CORIANDER: Cilantro, which is sometimes called coriander, is another wonderful leafy herb often used in Asian and Mexican cuisine. It is an acquired taste that people either love or hate. This may be due to the recipe that the cilantro is used in, or perhaps the amount used. It has a strong flavor and should be used sparingly. But its unique taste really adds character to many dishes. So if you've tried it before and didn't like it, I encourage you to try it again where indicated in my recipes. When I have the time, I like to remove the leaves from the stalks; this can be quite time consuming, however, so if you prefer, you can chop the stalks (at least the top tender portions) and the leaves together.

DILL: Dill is another of my favorite herbs. I use it in salad dressings, main dishes, tomato sauces, and to flavor grain and bean dishes. It works particularly well in dips and non-dairy creamy dressings, as well as with potatoes. To use dill, chop away the fine leaves with the fine, tender portions of the stalks. If your only previous experience with the flavor of dill is from pickles or other commercial "dill"-flavored items, you will be delighted at how appealing the flavor is in my recipes.

OREGANO: Oregano is a herb that people know well and use often in its dried form. Dried oregano is quite good for many dishes, particularly in Italian-inspired foods such as tomato sauces, lasagnas, and pizzas. Since the dried form is typically added early to the dish, the flavor can be imparted throughout the cooking time. Fresh oregano adds extra pizzazz to your favorite recipes that normally call for dried. A fairly strong herb, the leaves can be torn away from the stalks and chopped (the tender parts of the stalks can also be used). Whole stalks can be immersed in sauces or soups while they are simmering, and then removed before serving.

PARSLEY: There are several varieties of parsley, two of the most common being curly parsley and Italian flat-leaf parsley. Parsley is fairly robust, doesn't bruise as basil does, and keeps well in the refrigerator. You can use both the stems and the leaves. The stems have a stronger flavor, so you may want to reserve these for vegetable stocks, or chop the more tender part of the stalks along with the leaves. Parsley is a wonderful addition to many dishes, particularly when chopped fine and sprinkled to "finish," as well as on fresh salads.

ROSEMARY: Rosemary is a very strong herb, a small amount is all that's needed to impart flavor. As with oregano, you can easily immerse a full stalk of rosemary in soups, stocks, and sauces to draw out the flavor, and then remove the stalk before serving. To use the leaves, pull them away from the woody stalk (this is easiest to do by running your fingers down the length of the stalk in the opposite direction of the growth of the leaves), and then chop the desired amount.

TARRAGON: Tarragon has a slight aniseed (licorice) taste, and is often used to flavor vinegars and sauces. With this distinct flavor, it should be used somewhat sparingly initially to see how much of it you like. Tear the leaves away from the stalk and then chop to use in your dishes. The tender parts of the stalks can also be used.

THYME: Thyme is great in mushroom and potato recipes, as well as in many other vegetable dishes. If the stalks are fairly tough, remove the leaves from the stalks. As with rosemary, this is done easiest by running your fingers down the length of the stalk in the opposite direction of the growth of the leaves. However, if you have young thyme and the stalks are very tender (you will know because it will be somewhat tedious to remove the leaves), you can use both the leaves and the stems.

Grains and Flours

ARBORIO RICE: Arborio is an Italian rice, and the key ingredient for risotto recipes. It is a short, fat, pearly white grain that absorbs plenty of liquid and develops a wonderful, rich, and creamy texture. It is also good to use in rice pudding recipes. Arborio can be found in local grocery stores and specialty markets.

ARROWROOT FLOUR: Arrowroot flour, sometimes called arrowroot powder, can be found in health food stores. It is a natural, plant-based thickening agent, used as an alternative to cornstarch. A white powder that looks just like cornstarch, arrowroot flour can be substituted measure for measure.

CHICKPEA FLOUR: Chickpea flour, sometimes called garbanzo bean flour, is made by grinding chickpeas into a powdery texture. It can be found in health food stores and specialty markets carrying Italian ingredients. In the few recipes where I call for chickpea flour, other flours can be substituted.

COUSCOUS: Couscous is a pasta, made from wheat, very small and round in shape. It cooks quickly; most brands take just five minutes. It is available in regular and whole wheat varieties in grocery stores as well as health food stores.

KAMUT FLOUR: Kamut flour is made from a grain that is related to wheat, but offers more nutritional benefits, including higher protein, and is an alternative for people who have sensitivities to wheat. Kamut flour is somewhat coarse, with a light yellow color and a pleasant, nutty-sweet taste. Kamut flour as well as other Kamut-based products such as breads, cereals, and pastas, can be found in your health food store.

MILLET: Millet is round and similar in appearance to couscous, but a little larger and denser. Unlike couscous, millet is, in fact, a grain rather than pasta. It can be found in health food stores and some grocery stores.

PHYLLO PASTRY: Phyllo pastry is paper-thin and can be found in the freezer section of your grocery store. It usually comes in a long box with the phyllo rolled up inside, 24 or so sheets layered on top of one another. Keep it frozen until ready for use, then thaw it in the refrigerator overnight (or about 12 hours) for best results. (In a pinch, you can thaw it at room temperature for 2 to 4 hours the day of use, however, thawed this quickly the pastry can thaw unevenly and is not as easy to work with.) Phyllo seems fragile because it is papery thin and can tear, but it is also very forgiving, and any tearing and patching will not affect the final product. Work with a few sheets at a time, keeping the other sheets moist by covering them with a slightly damp towel (not wet). If the phyllo dries out (this usually happens around the edges), it will become brittle and crack, but if you work fairly quickly with it, it likely will not dry out. Any leftover sheets of phyllo can be tightly wrapped in plastic wrap and kept refrigerated for about a week. The phyllo pastry that I use is free of animal products but not all are, so you should check the list of ingredients on any you buy.

QUINOA: Quinoa (pronounced "keen-wah") is an ancient grain that is gaining in popularity. It cooks quickly and produces a light, couscous-like grain that is much higher in protein than other grains. You may find it in grocery stores in the rice or grains section, or in the ethnic/imported foods section. If not, you can definitely find it in health food stores. Other products using quinoa as the grain base, including cereals and pastas, are coming onto the market.

WILD RICE: Wild rice is actually a water-grown grass. It has a beautiful, dark purple-black color, a wonderfully nutty taste, and a slightly chewy texture. When you cook wild rice, the grain opens up, exposing the whitish interior. You may find wild rice in your local grocery store, and you can certainly find it in health food stores, sometimes also packaged with other grains as a wild rice mixture.

WHOLE WHEAT PASTRY FLOUR: Whole wheat pastry flour is a little finer in texture than regular whole wheat flour. As a result, baked goods using this flour are lighter. If you don't have whole wheat pastry flour, you can use regular whole wheat flour, substituting some unbleached all-purpose flour (about ¼-½ of the total amount) to lighten the texture.

Nuts and Seeds

ALMOND BUTTER (AND OTHER NATURAL NUT AND SEED BUTTERS): Similar to peanut butter, almond butter is made from ground almonds. Unlike most commercial peanut butters, natural nut butters are made purely from ground nuts, with no hydrogenated oils, additives, or sweeteners. You can purchase them in health food stores and some grocery stores. There are many varieties, including smooth and crunchy almond butters, cashew butter, sesame seed butter (tahini), and pumpkin seed butter. When you open the jars you will notice that the natural oils have risen to the top; this is simply because there are no additives to keep the oils suspended, and so they naturally rise. As the jar states, you need to mix the oil in with the butter to loosen and smooth it. Nut butters are delicious, and some, like almond butter, have a natural sweetness. Experiment and find your favorites!

FLAX SEEDS/FLAX MEAL: Flax seeds and flax meal can be purchased in the refrigerated section of health food stores (you need to keep it refrigerated). Flax meal, which I use the most in my recipes, is flax seeds that have been ground or crushed. It has a crumb-like texture, and works better for some baking purposes. In this form, its nutrients are better absorbed in our bodies than flax seeds. Raw flax seeds and flax oil are excellent sources of omega-3 fatty acids. Flax seed oil is also available in health food stores (again refrigerated). I do not use flax oil in these recipes, although it can be used as a substitute for some of the olive oil used in my salad dressing recipes. If you are unable to purchase flax meal, purchase the seeds whole and grind them in a coffee grinder or small processor. Flax meal is also excellent simply sprinkled on various dishes. It has a subtle, nutty flavor, so try blending it with fruit or soy milk smoothies, or sprinkling it on salads, bread/toast (on top of a spread or nut butter), cereals, and even on non-dairy ice creams and other desserts.

TAHINI: Tahini is made from sesame seeds, and is sometimes called sesame seed butter. It is similar to the texture of nut butters, and is a main ingredient in hummus recipes. Tahini works well in sauces, dressings, and as a binder for veggie burgers and some baked goods. It is often available in grocery stores among the peanut butters, and is also readily available in health food stores.

Soy Products

MISO: Miso is a fermented paste that is made either wholly from soybeans, or from soybeans combined with a grain such as brown rice or barley. There are different varieties of miso; the lighter colored varieties are generally milder in flavor and less salty than the darker types. In these recipes, I use a brown rice miso. It is light and mellow in color and taste, yet quite thick in texture, so works well as a binder and emulsifier. (It is also less expensive than some of the pure soybean versions.) You may want to experiment with your favorite miso in these recipes.

SOY MILK: Soy milk is made from soybeans which have been soaked in water, crushed, and then boiled. This process yields a pulp, which is made into tofu, and a milky liquid, which becomes soy milk. There are many brands and varieties of soy milk, which have become increasingly accessible in grocery and health food stores and have really improved in taste in recent years. I encourage you to try a few different brands until you find one that you really like. There are two types available. One comes in an aseptic container and typically has a shelf life of up to a year. The other must be kept refrigerated, and is usually found in the dairy sections of grocery stores. The refrigerated soy milks are what I use in my recipes. There are lower fat versions, and flavors such as vanilla, chocolate, carob, and strawberry. Some are also fortified with calcium and vitamins D and B_{12}. Rice and almond milks are also available in grocery and health food stores. I do not list these milks as ingredients in my recipes since I have tried to simplify the number and variety of ingredients for you to use, but you can experiment with them if you choose. I find that they aren't always as rich and smooth as soy milks, but in most cases they should substitute fine.

SOY/RICE CHEESES: There are several varieties and brands of soy and rice cheeses on the market, including "cheese" slices and parmesan, so you may want to experiment. Some are quite good. If you are a pure vegan, check the ingredients for those without casein. You can usually find these in the dairy or health food section of your grocery store as well as in health food stores.

TAMARI: Tamari is a sauce made from fermented soybeans. Unlike some soy sauces, tamari is a true "soy sauce," without the colorings, sweeteners, and chemicals in other commercial brands. Tamari is a wheat-free version of "shoyu," another traditional soy sauce made from fermented soybeans. It can be found in most grocery stores among the soy sauces, as well as in health food stores.

TOFU: Tofu is made from soybeans, and may be referred to as "bean curd" or "soy curd," although neither of these names is very appealing! The soybeans are soaked with water, then crushed and boiled. Through this process a milky liquid is formed, which is turned into soy milk. A pulp is also formed, which is processed further into tofu.

There are several brands of tofu on the market, as well as different varieties within the brands. Tofu comes in soft, medium, firm, and extra-firm textures. Within these textures you may also find different flavors, such as firm herb tofu, and "dessert" tofu. Dessert-style tofu is sweetened and very soft. You will also find varieties that are further reduced in fat and others that may be calcium fortified. (Tofu is not a good source of calcium unless it has been processed with calcium; this will be noted on the label.)

Tofu packaging also varies. It is available in aseptic containers that have a very long shelf life, or in sealed clear plastic packaging with tiny bubbles of water visible between the wrap and the tofu. The aseptic containers do not need to be refrigerated, so while you may find them in the dairy or refrigerated sections of your grocery store or health food stores, they may also be found on the shelves. The tofu sealed in clear plastic does not have as long a shelf life and must be refrigerated. I keep both types on hand, as well as a few different textures. Once you have opened a package of tofu, cover it with cold water and a tight lid or plastic wrap and refrigerate. Replace the water every day. The tofu should be used within 5-6 days. I try to use my tofu as soon as possible after opening, since I don't like to throw it away, and the process of replacing the water daily is almost impossible to remember (and a bit of a nuisance!).

The aseptic packages contain "silken" tofu. Silken tofu is smoother and silkier (hence the name) than the regular brands, the result of an alternative processing of the soy milk into bean curd. Soft and medium "silken" tofu is wonderful in dessert recipes and for puréeing, although regular soft and medium tofu can often be substituted. It is important to note that the extra firm "silken" tofu is not at all like the firm and extra-firm varieties of the regularly processed tofu, however. Therefore, where my recipes call for "extra-firm" tofu, I refer to the standard extra-firm tofu, unless the recipe specifically states "silken firm or extra-firm silken tofu."

The varieties of tofu offer endless options for recipe creations. Tofu is quite tasteless on its own, and so it will take on the flavors of your recipes. The soft and medium textures are excellent puréed for salad dressings, dips, and sauces, as well as in desserts. For baked goods, they can be used as egg replacers (use ¼ cup and purée or mash very well to replace one egg). The firm and extra-firm varieties are "meatier," so work best as a meat replacer. Mash or crumble it in chili and soups, and to make "meatballs" (or as I call them, "neat balls") and "burgers." It also absorbs marinades very well: cube, slice, or mash the tofu, marinate it, then fry or grill it. When using a marinade with firm or extra-firm varieties, I first freeze the tofu, then thaw it and squeeze out any extra liquid (as described in the section entitled "Everyday Cooking Tips and How-To's" – Preparing and Marinating Firm/Extra-Firm Tofu, p.31). The tofu absorbs marinades and other flavors much better, and has a denser, "meatier" texture.

I have surprised many guests with wonderful dishes using tofu, particularly desserts where people would never have guessed that the secret creamy ingredient is soft tofu! Experiment with it and you will see what a wonderful food tofu is to cook and bake with.

Spices, Seasonings, and Condiments

EGG-FREE, NON-DAIRY MAYONNAISE: Yes, it does exist, and you should be able to purchase various brands in health food stores and many grocery stores. I use a one called "Nayonnaise," a soy-based mayonnaise that tastes wonderful and is not too high in fat. Use it just as you would a regular mayonnaise, straight out of the jar for sandwiches or mixed with other ingredients for dips, dressings, and other dishes. If you are substituting another egg-free, non-dairy mayonnaise for Nayonnaise in my recipes, I suggest you use a brand that has a creamy texture with less of a "tangy" taste.

BALSAMIC VINEGAR: Balsamic vinegar is a dark brown, robust, sweet-sour Italian vinegar which can be found in grocery and specialty stores. There are higher grades of balsamic vinegar available in specialty shops; these can be very expensive, but are more syrupy in texture, and using just a few drops will enhance a final dish. In my recipes I use standard balsamic vinegars found in most grocery stores.

CHIPOTLE HOT SAUCE: I use this hot sauce in my recipes when I want to add a little heat and a smoky flavor. If you have a favorite hot sauce, you can substitute it for the chipotle sauce if you wish. A chipotle chile is actually a jalapeño chile that has been smoked and dried. The result is a very dark chile with a deep smoky taste. Chipotle hot sauces can be found in grocery stores as well as specialty markets.

FENUGREEK: Fenugreek is a spice used in Indian cuisine, often in curry spice mixtures. Bought whole, it is cube-shaped. It can be found in grocery stores (sometimes in the imported foods/ethnic foods sections), larger health food stores, and specialty markets.

HOISIN SAUCE: Hoisin sauce is a thick, dark, mildly spicy sauce with some sweetness. It typically contains soybeans, garlic, chiles, sugar, vinegar, and other seasonings. It adds wonderful flavor to stir-fries, salad dressings and marinades. It is found in small jars in the Asian/ethnic foods section of grocery stores, as well as specialty markets.

LEMONGRASS: Lemongrass looks somewhat like a scallion or green onion that is lighter green in color and much coarser in texture. It imparts a lemon flavor that is distinct from lemon itself, although lemon rind can often be used as a substitute. Use the whitish base portion, up to where the stalk becomes greener and coarser, and starts to branch. You will want to use mostly the inner layers, which are more tender than the outer ones. The best way to get to these layers is to smash the base of the lemongrass using the side of a large knife to flatten and open up the stalk somewhat. Cut off the base and discard some of the tough outer layers to reach the tender center, then chop for use in recipes. Lemongrass can be found in specialty markets and most grocery stores.

RED WINE VINEGAR: As its name suggests, this vinegar is made from red wine. It has a light red color, and is milder than white vinegar, with a pleasant flavor, and is most often used in salad dressings. It can be purchased in grocery stores.

RICE VINEGAR: Made from rice, this vinegar is milder and more flavorful than regular vinegar. There are two varieties, plain and seasoned. Seasoned rice vinegar is sweeter than the regular kind, as it is contains some sugar. It works nicely in different salad dressing recipes, although both varieties are wonderful and can easily be substituted for one another. It can be purchased in grocery stores, either in the Asian/ethnic foods section, or among the other vinegars.

SEA SALT: Sea salt is processed through the evaporation of sea water. Unlike regular table salt, sea salt contains no other additives such as iodine. Check the label when purchasing. It is available in most grocery stores as well as in health food stores.

Vanilla Beans: I use a vanilla bean in one recipe here, "Lusciously Light Tiramisu" (p. 194). For this dish, I wanted a strong vanilla flavor without the alcohol taste that too much pure vanilla extract can impart. This is achieved so well using a vanilla bean that I could not remove it from this one recipe, no matter how much I wanted to simplify the ingredient base. Vanilla beans can be purchased in specialty stores, health food stores, and usually in grocery stores. They should be soft, and packaged in an airtight container, and stored at room temperature. Vanilla beans can be sliced lengthwise and the wonderful aromatic seeds scraped from the shell. Alternatively, if you are warming or heating a mixture, you can place the entire bean in the liquid to allow the rich vanilla flavor to seep into your mixture.

Sweeteners and Chocolate

Blackstrap Molasses: Blackstrap molasses is slightly more bitter and stronger tasting than regular molasses, but it offers more nutritive value. It can usually be found in grocery stores, as well as health food stores. While blackstrap molasses is used in some recipes, it can be substituted with regular molasses.

Honey Options: If you are a pure vegan and do not include honey in your diet, you probably are already aware of sweeteners which can be used as alternatives to honey, such as brown rice syrup, barley malt, and agave nectar. I find agave nectar works particularly well as a honey alternative, with a similar sweetness and consistency. Of course, if you are not opposed to using honey, you can simply use it in any of my recipes where "honey option" is listed. You can find these sweeteners in health food stores and some grocery stores.

Chocolate and Chocolate Chips: People often ask me if I eat chocolate; it's true, I love chocolate – non-dairy, of course, which is not that difficult to find. If you look for chocolate in the baking section of grocery stores, you will find non-dairy chocolate chips, bars, and squares, typically labeled as "semi-sweet." Darker chocolate is usually non-dairy, but not always, so be sure to check the list of ingredients. My very favorite non-dairy dark chocolate is callebaut, which I purchase at local health food stores. The difference between the grocery store brands of dark chocolate and callebaut is quite noticeable. Callebaut chocolate is smoother and richer on the palate, and offers a deeper chocolate taste. It is fairly expensive, so if you want to indulge, perhaps buy some for that special dessert or as a fix for that persistent chocolate craving. If you prefer to use carob instead of chocolate, go ahead. But keep in mind that the final product will have a different taste.

STEVIA: Stevia is a herb which is incredibly sweet yet has no calories. It is completely natural, and is processed into powdered and liquid forms. A great alternative for people who have sugar sensitivities, but it must be used very sparingly because it is much, much sweeter than regular sugar; for instance, roughly one teaspoon of ground stevia is as sweet as about one cup of white sugar. Substituting stevia for sugar in recipes is not necessarily simple, however, since it will affect the volume of baked goods, and because too much can leave an aftertaste. I have listed some stevia options in the "Sweet Treat" recipes if you are interested in experimenting with this sweetener. You can find stevia in health food stores.

UNREFINED SUGAR: I use unrefined sugar instead of white or brown sugar in my sweet treat recipes (although these refined sugars can be substituted if desired). While you should not overdo the amount of sweets you eat in general, refined sugars are particularly unfavorable. They are nutritionally void and stress your digestive system. So I have looked for ways to create delicious sweet treats using such ingredients as maple syrup and unrefined sugar. Unrefined sugar can usually be found in grocery stores as well as in health food stores.

Everyday Cooking Tips and "How-To's"

As you go through individual recipes, you will notice that I give
detailed instructions about the preparation of ingredients, and notes
and ideas for substitutions and your own creativity. I have included as
much information as I can within the recipes to make it easy for you.
The following tips and "how-to's" are general and separate from
any specific recipe, to help you with everday cooking.

Preparing and Marinating Firm/Extra-Firm Tofu: Tofu is a mystery
to many people. "It tastes like nothing," many might say. Well, in fact, it does
generally taste like nothing straight out of the box. But this is the charm of
tofu. You can use it in anything from entrées to desserts, because the variety
of tofu textures lend themselves to different recipes, and the tofu itself takes on
the flavors of the different ingredients. In general, soft to medium tofu should
be used for dips, dressings, sauces, puddings, and in desserts as egg replacers
or for puddings. Firm and extra-firm tofu are best for entrées requiring a
"meaty" texture, such as stir-fries, "burgers," and chili. The firm and extra-firm
varieties absorb marinades very well, and can then be fried, grilled, or added to
sauces and soups. Silken tofu, which is packaged in aseptic containers, is
somewhat different. Both the soft and firm silken varieties work best in recipes
that are blended or puréed.

When marinating tofu, or mincing it for burgers or meat balls, it is best to
freeze it first (this is for regular firm/extra-firm tofu, not silken firm/extra-firm
tofu). When you are ready to use the tofu, let it thaw in the package at room
temperature (this will take six to seven hours to thaw all the way through).
You can speed the thawing process by placing the tofu, still in the package,
in a bowl of hot water, replacing the hot water several times; the tofu will thaw
within 30-40 minutes. Once thawed, remove the tofu from the package and
squeeze as much liquid out as possible. If you want to cube or slice the tofu,
try not to ruin the shape of the block too much while squeezing it. You can
first squeeze it with your hands over the sink, then wrapped in paper towels.

Removing this excess liquid will give the tofu a spongier, "meatier" texture, allowing it to more readily absorb flavors and marinades. (For an example of marinating and cooking tofu, see "Tasty Tofu Tidbits," p. 158). You can then cube, slice, or mash the tofu, depending on your recipe. While freezing and thawing the tofu will produce the best results for marinating it, if you haven't frozen the tofu, you can still squeeze out most of the liquid with good results.

CHOOSING POTATOES: When I first began to cook, I didn't realize the differences between varieties of potatoes other than the color. I started to learn about starchy and waxy potatoes, and this became very confusing, particularly when confronting the many varieties available in the grocery store. Here is some basic and practical information that should be helpful to you to understand some of the differences.

Starchy: Also referred to as mealy, these potatoes are high in starch with a low moisture content. Often used for baking, they become very fluffy and soft throughout, and also work well as french fries or mashed (although for those who prefer chunkier mashed potatoes, use lower starch potatoes). The Russet is the quintessential starchy potato.

All-purpose or medium starch: These potatoes are "middle of the road": they work well for many purposes, including baked, mashed, and fries, yet have enough structure that they can be used in dishes requiring a chunkier texture, such as salads. Many of my recipes call for all-purpose potatoes, to simplify your pantry ingredients. All-purpose potatoes may simply be marketed as white potatoes, and have a much thinner, lighter skin than a high starch Russet. The Yukon Gold is an example of an all-purpose, or medium starch potato.

Low starch: Also called waxy potatoes, these have a high water content and retain their shape and consistency when cooked, and are great for salads, boiling, and pan roasting. In comparing baked potatoes, the Russet when cut will be very fluffy, light, and almost crumbly, whereas the waxy potato will keep its shape and be more chunky in texture. Red and baby potatoes are examples of low starch, waxy potatoes, but white and Yukon Gold can easily be substituted.

YAMS: Any reference to yams in this book calls for the orange fleshed potatoes, sometimes called sweet potatoes. However, to avoid confusion, my recipes use the orange tubers most commonly known as yams, rather than potatoes that are sweeter in taste and more yellow in color, which are sweet potatoes.

CHOPPING AND MINCING GARLIC: To chop garlic, first remove the skin surrounding the clove. This is easily done by turning the blade of a large knife so that its side lays on the garlic clove, and then banging down on the blade side with your hand. The clove will "squish" somewhat, the skin will be very easy to remove, and the clove easier to chop. I also trim off the hard end of the clove, since it is not pleasant to bite into! A great trick for chopping garlic very fine is to use some salt as an abrasive agent. Using a good knife, sprinkle a pinch of sea salt over the cloves, and begin to mince the garlic. To chop the garlic as fine as pushing it through a garlic press, after chopping it with the salt, use some pressure to smear it across your cutting board with the side of your knife. Then run the sharp edge of the blade across the flattened garlic again, chopping it very fine. Repeat several times.

ROASTING GARLIC: Roasting garlic is very easy and produces a wonderful result. The cloves become soft, mild tasting, and a little sweet. Take two or more whole bulbs of garlic and with a sharp knife slice off the top of the bulb just so the cloves are exposed. Preheat oven to 400°F. Fold a large piece of tin foil and place the garlic bulbs in the center side by side. Drizzle the tops of the bulbs with a little olive oil, then fold the tin foil over so that the bulbs are completely covered. Bake for roughly 45-50 minutes, or until the cloves are very soft and have browned a little. Let cool enough to handle. Use a butter knife to remove each clove from the bulb. Or, even easier, turn the bulb upside down and squeeze the cloves out from the base of the bulb. I always roast more than I need for a recipe. Wrap them well in plastic and keep them in the refrigerator for quick use!

ROASTING PEPPERS: To roast red peppers, core them and then cut into quarters, lengthwise (or other large pieces). Remove any remaining seeds and white membranes on the underside of the pepper flesh. Line a baking sheet with parchment paper (you can lightly oil the sheet, but parchment paper is easier for clean up). Place the pepper pieces with the skin side up, and spritz or rub with some olive oil. Preheat the oven to broil, and broil the peppers for 13-15 minutes or longer, until the skins are blistering and have blackened in many spots. Once well blistered, remove the peppers and place in a clean bowl and then cover with plastic wrap, or place in a clean, sealed plastic bag. Let sit for another 15-20 minutes until cool enough to handle. Remove the peppers from the bowl or bag, and then peel away the skins from the flesh.

CLEANING MUSHROOMS: Mushrooms absorb water very easily, and for most recipes, you don't want this extra water seeping out of the mushrooms while they are cooking. So, rather than use water to clean them, use a clean cloth or paper towel. Lightly dampen the cloth or towel, so that practically no water can be squeezed from it. Gently brush your mushrooms with the cloth or towel, which will remove most of the dirt. I love portabella mushrooms in particular for their taste and versatility, but their undersides, or gills, can transfer a lot of black color to a dish, as well as house extra dirt. When I use portabellas, I gently scrape away the gills with a large spoon.

COOKING PASTA: When cooking pasta, note the suggested cooking time on the package; fresh pasta will take just a few minutes, while dried pasta can take anywhere from 4 to 10 minutes. A few pinches of sea salt should be added to the boiling water before adding the pasta. Pasta is best when cooked al dente, meaning firm to the bite. When cooking your pasta, test it, and if it is a little firm as you bite through it, drain it then. Keep in mind that it will continue to cook once you drain it and add it to your sauce. Avoid overcooking, as this will make the pasta mushy. When draining the pasta, do not rinse it before adding it to your sauce; the remaining starch on the pasta will be swept away if rinsed, and this starch helps the sauce to "bind" with the pasta.

When we serve pasta at home, my husband always jokes, "How many noodles do you want? Five or six?" Well, I'm not that extreme, but generally I do like to more sauce relative to the amount of pasta. This is typically opposite to how pasta is usually served; it's my "pasta peculiarity"! Because I adjust the amount of pasta I use depending on the sauce, the side dishes, or simply by the mood I am in, I do not list amounts of pasta to use in my recipes. In general, the pasta sauces will easily serve 3-4 people, so use your judgment on how much pasta you would like to have for your meal. Again, this may depend on what other items you are serving in your meal. I also love to experiment with the different types of cut pasta (penne, fusilli, radiatore, etc.) that you can purchase in vegetable and different grain blends.

COOKING WITH CANNED AND BOTTLED GOODS: There are several canned and bottled goods which I regularly stock in my pantry, including beans, artichokes, and tomatoes. These can be a good alternative to fresh ingredients; artichokes, for example, can be time-consuming, complicated, and expensive to use in fresh form, so their canned or bottled equivalent can usually meet your needs. It is important to rinse canned items such as artichokes and beans before using, to "freshen" them and remove excess sodium.

COOKING WITH FRESH AND DRIED HERBS: Fresh herbs are delightful, and I use them whenever possible. There are certain recipes for which dried herbs cannot be used as a substitution, where the fresh herb is the basis of the recipe; pesto is one example. There are times, however, when dried herbs substitute just fine.

When you want to substitute dried for fresh herbs, a good rule of thumb is to use roughly 1 teaspoon of the dried (leaves, as opposed to powdered) for 1 tablespoon of the fresh (roughly ⅓ the amount). If you are using powdered herbs, the flavor will be more intense than that of the dried leaves, so use less. Again, as an example, roughly ½ teaspoon of the powdered form for 1 tablespoon of the fresh.

Fresh herbs should be added towards the end of the cooking time so they don't lose their intensity with the heat. This is particularly true for chives and very leafy herbs such as basil, parsley, cilantro, and dill. Add these just a few minutes before serving the dish. Dried herbs, on the other hand, can be added in the earlier stages so that the flavors will be drawn out through the cooking time. Specific information on the fresh herbs used in these recipes is provided in the "Shopping for Everyday Ingredients" section, p.19.

COOKING WITH FRESH INGREDIENTS: Whenever possible I like to use fresh ingredients. While it may be convenient at times to use prepared foods, fresh ingredients really make the difference when creating a nutritious meal that tastes incredible. The freshness of produce and seasonings will add rich, deep flavors and textures to your meals, and will maximize nutritional benefits. Using fresh ingredients in your cooking can also make it easier to reduce the amount of fat because you have partially replaced the flavor enhancers of the fat component with the incredible flavors imparted by the fresh ingredients.

I find that certain ingredients, such as garlic, ginger, and lemon juice, are not easily substituted by prepared products (e.g., bottled minced garlic, bottled lemon juice). While these may come in handy in a pinch when you are very busy or unable to get to a market, wherever possible try to use these ingredients fresh.

COOKING WITH ORGANIC INGREDIENTS: Although my recipes do not specify organic produce or other organic ingredients, I do buy them regularly and cook with them as much as possible. Organic foods often have better flavor, and organic farming is better for our environment and produces more nutritious foods. For some, organic ingredients can be costly or difficult to access. But if organic products are not an option, there is no need to be concerned about the taste appeal of these recipes; they will still be delicious!

COOKING WITH SUN-DRIED TOMATOES: When using sun-dried tomatoes, I often reconstitute them first, soaking them in boiling water for 10-15 minutes. This makes them easier to eat, and softens their flavor. The exception is if I use them in a sauce such as a tomato pasta sauce; in this case I add them dried, as they will soften during the cooking. Some of my recipes call for sun-dried red peppers, with sun-dried tomatoes as a substitution. Sun-dried red peppers are similar to the tomatoes, and for most purposes you will want to reconstitute them. Sun-dried red peppers are delicious, and add more sweetness to a dish than sun-dried tomatoes.

MAKING BREADCRUMBS: Some of my recipes call for "good quality breadcrumbs." I do not like to use store-bought breadcrumbs because they are usually made from plain white bread. I prefer whole grain breads most of the time, for their taste, texture, and nutrition. I get great artisan breads from a local bakery and then freeze them. When I need breadcrumbs, I defrost the bread and crumble it using a food processor, which also allows you to control the size of your breadcrumbs.

MELTING CHOCOLATE: Chocolate burns easily, and so it is best not to melt it with direct heat from the stove or in the microwave. Instead, place it in a small bowl or saucepan over a larger saucepan of boiling water. The heat from the boiling water will melt the chocolate more evenly without the risk of it quickly burning. It is important not to drop any water into the melting chocolate … as little as one drop of water will make the chocolate seize up and become difficult to work with. So, if your water is boiling rapidly, reduce the heat a little and this will still melt the chocolate.

NO BUTTER, BUT ALSO NO MARGARINE: None of my recipes include butter or margarine. Where a fat is required, I have used some type of natural oil (e.g., olive, sesame, canola). Although margarine is acceptable in the definition of a vegan diet, I avoid hydrogenated and partially hydrogenated oils wherever possible, and have therefore eliminated margarine from my diet.

TOASTING NUTS AND SEEDS: Toasting nuts and seeds enhances their flavors. As well, if fat content is a concern for you, toasting nuts is helpful because you get more intense flavor and can therefore use less in a recipe. Toasting is simple, particularly if you have a toaster oven (especially for small quantities). Place the nuts or seeds on the toaster oven tray, and bake until they turn a golden brown color and a "roasted" aroma is present. Keep a close eye on them, however, as they take only a few minutes to toast and can burn very quickly. If you don't have a toaster oven, place the nuts or seeds on a baking sheet and bake in the oven at around 400°F. Again, watch closely so they don't burn.

MENU PLANS AND QUICK MEAL IDEAS

I love this section. The Menu Plans are collections of recipes I think work
best together to make perfect meals for dinner parties, holidays, or when
you have more time to prepare a full menu, which generally is just once
in a while for most people. The Quick Meal Ideas offer some practical tips
for day-to-day meal preparations, and then some suggestions are given
for informal get-togethers such as picnics, potlucks, and kids' birthday parties.

Menu Plans

Here are some complete menu plans for special meals with family or friends. For the last menu suggestion, the Holiday Feast Menu, I include notes to help your cooking preparations. This menu is absolutely wonderful for holiday dinners, such as Christmas or New Year's. I have been preparing it for a number of years, and it is always a hit!

MENU 1: "Sweet and Sour Neat Balls" (p. 138), served over "Baked Herbed Spaghetti Squash" (p. 146), or a cooked grain such as basmati or wild rice, with a nice green salad topped with "Sesame Lemon Vinaigrette" (p. 81). A nice dessert to follow is "Baked Lime (or Lemon!) Cream Pie" (p. 190).

MENU 2: Serve either "Mediterranean Tortilla Pizzas" (p. 129) or "Mediterranean Sauce" (over pasta) (p. 108) along with a generous "Amazing Creamy Caesar Dressing" salad (complete with croutons) (p. 75), and "Why Deny? Ice Cream Pie" (p. 198) for dessert!

MENU 3: "Ginger Hoisin Rice Noodles" (p. 126) is a wonderful entrée with noodles and crisp veggies all in one. Serve "Puréed Roasted Parsnip and Fennel Soup" (p. 86) as an appetizer along with some crusty bread or "Flatbread" (p. 67). Follow this meal with "Blueberry-Orange Crisp Cake" (p. 192) topped with "Almond Whipped Cream" (p. 172), or a non-dairy vanilla ice cream.

MENU 4: "Mushroom Pecan Burgers" (p. 114), topped with "Mi-So Good Gravy!" (p. 72). Serve with "Roasted Baby Potatoes" (p. 152) and a crisp salad on the side topped with "Basic Balsamic Vinaigrette" (p. 76). A light, vibrant dessert would be nice after this meal, such as an assortment of sorbets or non-dairy ice creams. You could make "Banana Ice Cream" (p. 173) and/or "Mango Ice Cream" (p. 177), and serve in small scoops along with one or two store-bought sorbets.

MENU 5: Serve pasta tossed with either "Roasted Red Pepper Sauce" (p. 109), or "Best-o Pesto Sauce" (p. 104). Add a mixed greens salad on the side, tossed with "Sweet Red Wine Vinaigrette" (p. 82), or a side veggie such as "Quick Asparagus Sauté" (p. 150). Also include "Best Bruschetta" (p. 60) for a zesty and hearty side bread. For dessert, serve "Triple Layer Chocolate Cream Cake" (p. 196).

MENU 6: Serve "Lightened-Up Falafels" (p. 113) topped with "Tahini-Tamari Sauce" (p. 74), with "Sweet and Simple Grain Pilaf" (p. 157) and "Quick Roast Green Beans and Peppers" (p. 151) (or a salad). For dessert, serve "Coconut Cream Pie" (p. 193) or "Apple Cherry Crisp" (p. 189), topped with "Almond Whipped Cream" (p. 172) or a non-dairy vanilla ice cream.

MENU 7: HOLIDAY FEAST MENU

The recipes for this wonderful feast are:

- "Spiced Mushroom Potato Phyllo Pie" (p. 136)

- "All-Dressed Squash" (p. 118)

- "Mushroom Gravy" (p. 73)

- Several side dishes, including "Yam Purée" (p. 159), "Roasted Turnip Purée" (p. 155), "Roasted Carrots and Parsnips" (p. 153) and "Lightly Sautéed Kale" (p. 148)

- "Lusciously Light Tiramisu" (p. 194)

- Don't forget to serve some cranberry sauce with the menu!

Pulling all of these recipes together for one feast admittedly involves a good deal of preparation. Here are a few helpful tips:

- Have all of your ingredients on hand. Make a list and get everything a couple of days ahead, if possible.

- Prepare "Lusciously Light Tiramisu" a day or two in advance. Cover tightly with plastic wrap and refrigerate, preferably in an area without strong odors present (e.g., onions).

- "Spiced Mushroom Potato Phyllo Pie" can also be prepared a day in advance. Cover it tightly with plastic wrap and refrigerate.

- Prepare breadcrumbs for "All-Dressed Squash" the night before.

- Wash vegetables the night before or in the morning (e.g., the kale can be washed and chopped and refrigerated, as can the carrots and parsnips, kept in a bowl of water).

- When preparing ingredients, check which other recipes require the same ingredients, and prepare them at the same time. For instance, I prepare "All-Dressed Squash" and "Mushroom Gravy" on the day of the feast. I cut all the onion needed and divide it for each recipe. If making "Mushroom Gravy" and "Spiced Mushroom Potato Phyllo Pie" on the same day, do the same thing for the mushroom and onion preparation.

- Find some helpers and "sous chefs" to assist with vegetable cleaning, chopping, and definitely for clean-up!

Quick Meal Ideas

Often, the key to preparing quick meals is having leftovers such as potatoes, rice, or pasta, as well as some fresh veggies and a pantry stocked with prepared goods. For instance, keep some good quality canned or frozen veggie chilis on hand that can be quickly defrosted and heated. Similarly, when incorporating soups into meals, you can use stored homemade soups, or even easier, keep some good canned and boxed liquid soups on hand. There are excellent boxed non-dairy puréed soups available on the market now that work wonders as sauces and flavorings for quick meals.

POTATOES: Potatoes are wonderfully versatile, and very substantial as the cornerstone of quick meals, such as the following:

When baking potatoes, bake extra and store them in the fridge (leave skins on). Then, try some of these ideas:

- Slice thickly and fry in olive oil in a skillet over medium heat until crispy and seared a little. Season them with sea salt and fresh ground black pepper, or try chili powder, dried herbs, paprika, and/or cumin. Serve them with soup, salad, or as a side dish. They are great served with "Mi-So Good Gravy" (p. 72) or "Creamy Dijon Dill Dressing" (p. 77), or just vinegar or ketchup.

- Use hummus, veggie dips, sautéed vegetables, or veggie chilis to dress-up your baked potatoes. Either reheat the potatoes and simply top them with one or more of these add-ons, or scoop out some of the potato flesh, stuff the skins, top with some soy parmesan, if desired, and bake until bubbly. You can use the scooped-out potato flesh to make a potato salad (using a non-dairy, egg-free mayonnaise). Or, mash the potato flesh with some olive oil, salt, pepper, and soy milk, then re-stuff the potato skins, and top as you please!

- Cube the potatoes and toss into a veggie stir-fry.

- Cube the potatoes and sauté with veggies, cooked beans, and seasonings in olive oil. As an option, top with heated spaghetti sauce, fresh herbs, and a drizzle of olive oil.

When making mashed potatoes, do a large batch and store the extra in the fridge. Or you can make mashed potatoes with leftover boiled or baked potatoes (mashing in olive oil, soy milk, salt and pepper). Then try some of these ideas:

- Place some prepared veggie chili on the bottom of a casserole dish. Top with the mashed potatoes and bake until hot and the mashed potatoes have turned a golden brown.

- Reheat your mashed potatoes as a base (in place of rice or pasta) for a veggie stir-fry, or to be topped with soup.
- Make your mashed potatoes the center of your meal by adding in such ingredients as chopped artichoke hearts (from a can or jar), reconstituted sun-dried tomatoes, frozen corn kernels or other small frozen veggies, and roasted or chopped garlic. Either place in a lightly oiled casserole dish and top with breadcrumbs or soy parmesan and bake, or reheat and serve with a salad, steamed or sautéed veggies, or a light soup.

Follow the ideas given in the recipes for "Herbed Potato and Yam Fries" (p. 147), "Potato Chippers" (p. 149), and "Roasted Baby Potatoes" (p. 152), for other quick and easy ways to bake up tasty potatoes and fries.

RICE: Use leftover rice to create the following quick meals:

- Make burger patties, mixing in cooked beans, vegetables, and seasonings, and tahini or miso as binders, such as the recipe "Next-Day Rice (or other grain) Patties" (p. 115). You can use your own favorite vegetables and seasonings to put together quick patties, and serve with a sauce or gravy.
- Use rice as a base for soups and chilis. Reheat the rice and place a scoop in a bowl, and top with soup or veggie chili.
- Make a quick pilaf with leftover rice. Sauté onions and/or garlic in olive oil, followed with fresh veggies. Once the veggies are nicely sautéed, toss in the rice with some extra olive oil. If you want to add sauce, try a pasta sauce or one of the boxed puréed liquid soups, such as creamy mushroom, corn, or tomato. Fresh herbs add wonderful flavor.
- Make some rice wraps! Warm some flour tortillas, reheat the rice, and spread a layer in the center of the tortilla. Top with chopped raw veggies and herbs, or sautéed veggies, along with some chutney or salsa, or a vinaigrette or other sauce. Fold in the base and sides of your tortilla, and enjoy! (This works best with a stickier, shorter grain rice; "wrapping" your tortilla will be easier if it isn't overstuffed!)
- For many of these ideas, you can do the same thing with other leftover grains, including couscous, millet, and quinoa.

PASTA: Pasta is very versatile. It is useful to have extra cooked pasta in the fridge for dishes like pasta salads or quick soups. However, it is so easy to throw together a quick and wonderful meal with dry pastas that you should keep plenty on hand in your pantry, along with ingredients for sauces. Look for dry pastas that cook relatively quickly. Then, while the water boils and the pasta cooks, you can prepare your sauce.

People often wonder how to make their own sauce rather than using prepared ones. The new boxed puréed soups, mentioned above, work amazingly well as pasta sauces. For instance, you can use a non-dairy creamy mushroom soup mixed with sautéed fresh mushrooms, onions, and garlic, adding fresh herbs and soy parmesan for an extra flavor boost. There are many varieties of these soups which can be combined with many different ingredients to come up with really quick, delicious pasta meals. Other supplies needed for quick pasta sauces are:

- canned diced tomatoes

- vegetable broth

- good quality olive oil and some flavored olive oils

- kalamata or black olives

- sun-dried tomatoes and/or sun-dried red peppers

- artichoke hearts (canned or bottled)

- capers

- dried herbs and seasonings, such as oregano, basil, and chili powder

- white wine (sauté the wine with other ingredients to burn off the alcohol)

- soy parmesan

- fresh herbs

- frozen vegetables, such as peas and broccoli

- fresh vegetables, such as tomatoes, peppers, zucchini, carrots

- canned beans

- fresh garlic and onions

To make a quick but tasty tomato-based sauce, first sauté chopped garlic and onions in some olive oil over medium-low heat with a few pinches of salt and fresh ground pepper. Drain a large can of diced tomatoes and add in before the garlic takes on any color. Increase the heat to medium, and add dried spices and herbs, such as basil, oregano, and a little chili powder. Let this cook together for 7-8 minutes. Adjust the seasoning if desired. Add a little wine if you like, then increase the heat to burn off the alcohol. Toss in cooked pasta, then finish the sauce with some fresh herbs, extra olive oil, and/or soy parmesan. You can embellish this basic sauce by first sautéing some fresh vegetables with the garlic before adding the tomatoes, or by adding more delicate vegetables towards the end of the cooking, such as fresh spinach and/or frozen peas. Flavor can also come from adding chopped kalamata olives or drained capers. Don't forget that good quality bottled pasta sauces can also quickly be jazzed up with fresh herbs, capers or olives, or chopped fresh vegetables.

Picnics, Potlucks, and Kids' Birthday Parties

PICNICS: Sandwiches and salads are always great items for picnics, as well as muffins, snack loaves, and puddings. Some of the recipes that work great for picnic take-alongs are:

- "Divine Tofu Spread and Dip" (p. 61). Either make sandwiches using this as the filling, or bring it along with some pita breads, crackers or nacho chips.

- "Egg-less Sandwich Filling" (p. 99), and/or "Marinated Tofu Sandwich Filling" (p. 102). Use these as sandwich fillings, or bring along with pita breads, crackers, or nacho chips.

- "Lentil Veggie Wraps" (p. 101). Wrap each individually in plastic wrap.

- "Roasted Potato Salad" (p. 95). This salad is delicious either cold or at room temperature, so is a great picnic item. You can also use pasta in place of potatoes, as suggested in the recipe. Since the pasta/potatoes will soak up the olive oil as the salad sits, you may want to add a little extra oil before packing.

- If you enjoy veggie/rice/bean patties served cold or at room temperature, bring along the "Black Bean Millet Patties" (p. 110), or the "Lentil Miso Patties" (p. 112). Cook in advance, let cool, and then pack.

- For sweeter items, any of the muffins or snack loaves will pack well (slice the snack loaves in advance). Also, kids will love individually packed servings of "EVAN-illa Rice Pudding" (p. 175), or "Tropical Rice Pudding" (p. 178). Don't forget to bring along some cookies, too!

Here are some other quick ideas for making sandwiches and snacks for picnics:

- Make sandwiches with prepared hummus and sliced veggies such as lettuce, red pepper, cucumber, and avocado. You may want to pack the veggies separately and add them to your sandwiches at the picnic so that the bread doesn't get soggy. Pitas work great as well – everyone can stuff their own with their favorite veggies. You may want to bring along a small container of non-dairy, egg-free mayonnaise as well.

- If you have a favorite commercially prepared veggie burger, cook a few in advance. I particularly like Amy's California Burgers, and normally cook one or two extra whenever we have them. Fry patties in a pan coated with just a touch of oil. Once cooked, brush them with a little barbecue sauce, and refrigerate the extra patties. Later, mash the patties with Nayonnaise (or another non-dairy, egg-free mayonnaise), a little mustard and/or vegetarian worcestershire sauce, and diced veggies such as celery, bell peppers, and reconstituted sun-dried tomatoes. This makes a great sandwich filling. Bring along lettuce leaves and sliced tomatoes to finish your picnic sandwiches.

- The old stand-by – PB&J – is another great picnic item. Try some different versions using a natural nut butter like almond butter, and just a little jam or fruit spread, or some sliced bananas. Sprinkle a little cinnamon on the nut butter for an added twist.

- Prepared hummus or dips along with small pita pockets, sliced pita breads, crackers, chips, and fresh vegetable "sticks" are also great quick items.

POTLUCKS: For potlucks, it's great to have items completely prepared in advance, or which need just a little reheating when you arrive at the host's home. The following are great examples:

- Dips such as "Artichoke Delight Dip" (p. 58), "Roasted Red Pepper Dip" (p. 65), or "Roasted Eggplant Dip" (p. 64). Prepare in advance, and bake it once you arrive, or pre-bake almost fully, then finish baking at the potluck. Good with side breads or chips, such as those suggested in the recipes.

- "Artichoke Puffs" (p. 59), "Mexican Tortilla Triangles" (p. 63), or "Super Stuffed Mushrooms" (p. 66). Prepare these tasty appetizers in advance, bring them along on your baking sheets, and cook them when you arrive.

- Soups are wonderful, since they can be made ahead of time, then reheated. Hearty soups are particularly good, including "Chickpea Mash Stew" (p. 84), "Spicy Thai Stew" (p. 88), and "Wild Rice and Mushroom Stew" (p. 91). "Soul-Full Veggie Bean Chili" (p. 87) is also great, served with nacho chips and guacamole.

- Casserole dishes work nicely, including "Carrot Zucchini Crumb Casserole" (p. 120), "Grate Potato Bake" (p. 128) (bring along a suggested sauce to serve with it), "Tomato-Olive Rice Bake" (p. 143), or "Cornmeal Chili Bake" (p. 122). All of these can be pre-baked before going to the potluck, and reheated later. Or, if you have time, you can completely bake them at the party.

- Other great recipes for potlucks include a salad with the "Amazing Creamy Caesar Dressing" (p. 75), as the dressing is so plentiful you can make a huge salad for the potluck, and "Mexican Tofu Tacos" (p. 130), since everyone can scoop filling into their own taco shells and top with whatever they like!

- Great dessert items include "Baked Lime (or Lemon!) 'Cream' Pie" (p. 190), "Coconut 'Cream' Pie" (p. 193), "Lusciously Light Tiramisu" (p. 194), and "Triple Layer 'Cream' Cake" (p. 196) (you can also make cupcakes from this recipe instead of a cake).

- Of course, cookies are always a hit. Favorites include "Coconut Raspberry Squares" (p. 182), "Hint O' Cinnamon Chocolate Chippers" (p. 184), "Double Chocolate Pecan Chippers" (p. 183), "Marie's More-ish Brownies" (p. 185), and "Ooey-Gooey Caramel Chip Bars" (p. 187).

KIDS' BIRTHDAY PARTIES: These ideas can be used for birthday parties, or just for fun meals for children:

- Kids love finger foods, so for healthier versions of fries, have them try "Potato Chippers" (p. 149), "Herbed Potato and Yam Fries" (p. 147), and "Roasted Baby Potatoes" (p. 152).

- Veggie burgers and veggie dogs are great for birthday parties. Top them with soy cheese slices, and whatever condiments they like.

- "Grilled Soy Cheese Sandwiches" (p. 100), are also great snacks or meals for kids. You may want to omit some of the veggies that are included in the recipe, particularly the green onions. Some kids love red peppers, though, so you may be able to keep these in, or sneak in other veggies that they like!

- Pizzas are always a hit, and can be whipped up quickly with prepared pizza crusts or even flour tortilla shells (follow the directions in "Mediterranean Tortilla Pizzas" (p. 129) for crisping up the shells). Top the shells with good quality pasta sauce or a pizza sauce, followed by soy mozzarella and/or soy parmesan, and some of your kids' favorite toppings, including veggies or soy deli meats (e.g., soy pepperoni).

- For a super birthday cake or cupcakes, use the "Triple Layer Chocolate "Cream" Cake" (p. 196). Decorate with candies or sprinkles, or whatever you like!

- "Why Deny? Ice-Cream Pie" (p. 198) will also be a hit with kids, as will the "Coconut Cream Pie" (p. 193).

- For a dessert (or a snack), "EVAN-illa Rice Pudding" (p. 175), "Tropical Rice Pudding" (p. 178), and "Banana Ice Cream" (p. 173), will be favorites!

- Cookies that kids will love at parties (or any other time) include "Ooey-Gooey Caramel Chip Bars" (p. 187), "Hint O' Cinnamon Chocolate Chippers" (p. 184), "Chewy Nutty Cereal Chip Squares" (p. 180), and "Swallow-It-All Banana Balls" (p. 188).

NO NEED FOR EVERYDAY CONCERNS

Have you ever noticed that reports on reducing the risk for various illnesses and diseases almost always highlight the importance of eating more fruits, vegetables, whole grains, beans, and nuts? I have yet to hear any such report say, "Now, be sure to increase your saturated fat and cholesterol while reducing your fiber by consuming more meat, chicken, eggs and dairy"! We repeatedly hear the importance of increasing our intake of plant based foods, yet very few of us do so.

We are bombarded with messages from meat and dairy industries to consume meat for protein and dairy for calcium. It is no surprise, then, that people who eat vegan foods on a regular basis are often questioned about their diet lacking in such things as protein, calcium, and iron. It has always amused me that meat-eaters are rarely questioned about their intake of vitamins and fiber, or told that they should be concerned about consuming too much protein, saturated fats, and cholesterol.

The idea that the vegan diet is intrinsically deficient in protein, calcium, and iron is an unfortunate myth in our culture. Certainly, if you eat vegan foods without a wide variety or are simply eating a lot of junk, your diet will be deficient, but this is true for anyone with unbalanced, unhealthy diets.

However, for those of you worried about protein, calcium, iron, and B_{12} in the vegan diet, these issues are addressed below. I am not a dietician or nutritionist, so statistical information referenced from secondary sources is provided. I also briefly cover the issue of heart disease, since it is the number one killer of both men and women of all racial and ethnic groups.[1]

Protein and Calcium

Protein is formed from amino acids, of which there are twenty-two. Our bodies make thirteen of these, and we need to get the remaining nine from food. While no single plant source contains all of these nine amino acids, we can obtain all of them by eating a variety of plant foods.[2] It is not necessary to worry about combining foods for adequate protein intake, as was once thought.[3] We simply need to obtain all of the nine amino acids over the course of a day or two, rather than within an hour of each other.[4]

Protein is found in all foods except fruits, fats, and sugars, so it is practically impossible not to meet or exceed the U.S. recommended dietary allowance.[5] Most people on a meat-based diet consume three to ten times more protein than their bodies need![6] Our real concern should not be the perceived lack of protein in a vegan diet, but rather for the over-consumption of protein in a typical North American diet.

High-protein diets in general, and meat-based diets in particular, lead to a decrease in bone density, producing the ongoing development of osteoporosis.[7] This is because when there is too much acid in our blood, the body withdraws calcium from the bones to balance the pH level. Animal foods are the most acid-forming foods, and can cause calcium to be drawn from the bones. Most fruits and vegetables, however, are base-forming, and so require no depletion of calcium stores in our bodies.[8]

It is interesting to note that despite the recommendations to consume more dairy products for calcium, societies with little or no consumption of dairy products and animal protein show a low incidence of osteoporosis.[9] Milk is touted for the prevention of osteoporosis, yet research indicates otherwise. A study following more than 75,000 women for 12 years showed no protective effect of increased milk consumption on fracture risk.[10] In fact, increased intake of calcium from dairy products was associated with a higher fracture risk.[11]

Other research shows a significant correlation between a high consumption of fruit and vegetables and bone health. Potassium and magnesium are strongly concentrated in many fruits and vegetables, and these nutrients were found to be very important to healthy bones, while consumption of dairy products was not.[12] You can decrease your risk of osteoporosis by reducing sodium and animal protein in the diet,[13,14,15] increasing your intake of fruits and vegetables,[16] and exercising.[17]

Some plant-based sources of calcium include dried fruits, almonds, walnuts, sesame seeds, celery, bran, cabbage, beans, string beans, oatmeal, barley, yams, cranberries, blackstrap molasses, olives, onions, dark greens (such as kale, swiss chard, collard greens, turnip greens, and mustard greens), broccoli, and sea vegetables, as well as calcium-fortified juices, tofu, soy milks, and rice milks.[18,19,20,21]

Iron

The belief that vegetarians tend to be anemic is common; however, studies have shown that they suffer less anemia than meat eaters.[22] Long-term studies indicate no iron deficiencies in lacto-ovo (consumption of milk and eggs) or pure vegetarian diets.[23] If you eat a diet rich in whole grains and legumes and eat five servings of fruits and vegetables a day, making sure your produce is of varying colors, you'll be assured of getting the amount of iron you need.[24]

Iron absorption is greatly assisted by vitamin C. Fresh vegetables and fruits are the best sources of vitamin C, whereas meats, dairy products, and eggs provide none.[25] Adding foods such as orange juice, cranberry juice, strawberries, cantaloupe, broccoli or tomatoes to each meal will boost your iron absorption.[26]

Plant-based sources of iron include members of the dried bean family (especially lentils, kidney beans, and lima beans), leafy greens, broccoli, prunes and prune juice, beets, peanut butter, sesame seeds, tofu, peas, and iron-fortified flour or whole grain-based products like breads and cereals.[27]

Vitamin B_{12}

The risk of developing health problems from low B_{12} intake is extremely small. Although animal foods contain B_{12}, this vitamin is actually produced in the plant kingdom.[28] When our foods were grown without chemicals, we got B_{12} from soil particles clinging to vegetables pulled from the ground, as well as through water from streams and wells. Today, however, our vegetables and water are no longer reliable sources of B_{12}, since we sterilize everything with chemicals.[29]

B_{12} deficiency is rare among vegetarians. This may be because B_{12}-forming bacteria are found in the human mouth and intestine, and most people store a 20-to-30-year supply of B_{12} in their bodies.[30] It may also be surprising that, although animal foods contain B_{12}, most cases of B_{12} deficiency occur among non-vegetarians. In these cases, the deficiency usually has to do with a person's inability to absorb the vitamin.[31]

The fact that today's plant-based diet contains no natural B_{12} is not an argument against vegan diets. Rather, it is a reminder of the nutritional price paid for how we have treated our food and water supplies over the years. Vegans now have to add back the B_{12} that has been lost.[32]

B_{12} can be obtained by adding a non-animal vitamin supplement to your diet.[33] As well, many foods are fortified with B_{12}, including some breakfast cereals, pastas, crackers, breads, soy milks, textured vegetable protein, and nutritional yeast.[34]

Heart Disease

Consider some of these startling statistics about heart disease:

- It is the leading cause of death among men and women between 35 to 74 years of age.[35]
- More than 2,500 Americans die each day of heart disease.[36]
- According to the American Heart Association, one of us has a heart attack every 20 seconds, and every 60 seconds one of us dies from one.[37]
- Women actually die at a higher rate from heart attacks than men do (53 vs. 47 percent). Signs of heart disease are found in 1 in 9 women aged 45 to 64, and in 1 in 3 women over 65. [38]

Now, consider some of these statistics:

- The primary culprits in heart disease are saturated fats found in meat, poultry, dairy products, and tropical oils, and the trans-fatty acids in margarine, fried foods, most commercial snacks, and packaged bakery products.[39]
- Heart disease mortality rates for vegetarians consuming eggs and dairy are only one-third that of meat eaters. Pure vegetarians (vegans) have only one-tenth the heart disease death rate of meat-eaters.[40]
- The amount you reduce your risk of heart attack by reducing your consumption of meat, dairy products, and eggs:

  reduce by 10%:   9% reduction of heart attack risk;
  reduce by 50%:   45% reduction of heart attack risk;
  reduce by 100%: 90% reduction of heart attack risk![41]

While diet is not the only lifestyle factor affecting heart disease, the statistics listed above show that it plays a crucial role. Fortunately, years of research by Dr. Dean Ornish have shown that a well-balanced vegetarian diet is beneficial not only for what it doesn't give you (unwanted cholesterol and saturated fat) but also for the protection it offers through its thousands of nutritious substances.[42] Dr. Ornish has shown that fruits, vegetables, nuts, and whole grains keep your heart in good shape.

[1]"Healthy Living, Healthy Heart," *Vegetarian Times*, February 2000.

[2]Ornish, Dr. Dean, *Dr. Dean Ornish's Program for Reversing Heart Disease*, 1990, p. 251.

[3]"Shattering the Myth of Protein," *Vegetarian Times*, March 1995.

[4]Ibid.

[5]Ibid.

[6]"Want Long Life? Lay Off Meat," *Tucson Citizen*, October 4, 1991.

[7]Robbins, John, *Diet for a New America*, 1987, p. 193.

[8]Ibid., pp. 196-197.

[9]McDougall, John A., M.D., and Mary A., *The McDougall Plan*, 1983, p. 52.

[10]Feskanich, D.; Willet, W.C.; Stampfer, M.J.; and Colditz, G.A. "Milk, dietary calcium, and bone fractures in women: a 12-year prospective study." *American Journal of Public Health*, 1997, 87:992-7.

[11]Cumming, R.G. and Klineberg, R.J. "Case-control study of risk factors for hip fractures in the elderly." *American Journal of Epidemiology*, 1994, 139:493-505.

[12]"Dietary influences on bone mass and bone metabolism: further evidence of a positive link between furit and vegetable consumption and bone health?" *American Journal of Clinical Nutrition*, Vol. 71, No. 1, 142-151.

[13]Finn, S.C. "The skeleton crew: is calcium enough?" *Journal of Women's Health*, 1998, 7(1):31-6.

[14]Nordin, C.B.E. "Calcium and osteoporosis." *Nutrition* 1997, 3(7/8):664-86.

[15]Reid, D.M. and New, S.A. "Nutritional influences on bone mass." Proceed., Nutritional Society, 1997;56:977-87.

[16]Tucker, K.L.; Hannan, M.F.; Chen, H.; Cupples, L.A.; Wilson, P.W.F.; and Kiel, D.P. "Potassium, magnesium, and fruit and vegetable intakes are associated with greater bone mineral density in elderly men and women." *American Journal of Clinical Nutrition*, 1999, 69:727-36.

[17]Prince, R.; Devine, A.; Dick, I, et al. "The effects of calcium supplementation (milk powder or tablets) and exercise on bone mineral density in postmenopausal women." *J Bone Miner Res*, 1995, 10:1068-75.

[18]"Strong bones without dairy," *Vegetarian Times*, March 1998.

[19]"What's Up with Calcium?" *Mothering*, March 1998.

[20]"Skeleton Crew," *Vegetarian Times*, July 1999.

[21]J.A.T. Pennington, *Bowes and Church's Food Values of Portions Commonly Used* (Philadelphia: J.B. Lippincott, 1994).

[22]Robbins, John, *Diet for a New America*, 1987, p. 297.

[23]Ibid., p. 300.

[24]"All About Iron," *Vegetarian Times*, April 1999.

[25]Robbins, John, *Diet for a New America*, 1987, p. 299.

[26]"All About Iron," *Vegetarian Times*, April 1999.

[27]Ibid.

[28]"Don't Be Baffled by B_{12}," *Vegetarian Times*, June 1995.

[29]Ibid.

[30]Ibid.

[31]"Don't Be Baffled by B_{12}," *Vegetarian Times*, June 1995.

[32]Ibid.

[33]"Ask. Dr. McDougall," *Veggie Life*, Winter 1999-2000.

[34]"Don't Be Baffled by B_{12}," *Vegetarian Times*, June 1995.

[35]"Healthy Living, Healthy Heart," *Vegetarian Times*, February 2000.

[36]Ibid.

[37]"The Heart of the Matter," *Vegetarian Times*, February 1999.

[38]Ibid.

[39]Ibid.

[40]Robbins, John, *Diet for a New America*, 1987, p. 215.

[41]EarthSave International, *Our Food Our World*, 1992.

[42]"The Heart of the Matter," *Vegetarian Times*, February 1999.

Recipe Listing

Note: Nutritional analysis is given for each recipe, denoted with ♥, based on average values for the ingredients involved. Different brands and varieties of ingredients may yield different nutritional analyses. Where a range of an ingredient is involved (e.g., 1-2 tbsp of olive oil), the analysis is based on the greater amount (e.g., 2 tbsp of olive oil rather than 1).

SIMPLE SIDES

MUFFINS AND SNACK LOAVES

Appetizers and Munchies

Artichoke Delight Dip

½ cup	soft tofu, packed
¼ cup	Nayonnaise (or other creamy, not too tangy vegan mayonnaise)
2-3	small to medium garlic cloves, roughly chopped
1 tbsp	lemon juice, fresh squeezed
2 tsp	rice vinegar
⅛ tsp	sea salt
	fresh ground black pepper to taste
1 can	artichoke hearts, rinsed well and drained (roughly 1 cup, coarsely chopped)
½ cup	fresh spinach, roughly chopped, packed (see sidebar)
3-4 tbsp	fresh parsley, chopped
2½ tbsp	soy/rice parmesan
½ tbsp	soy/rice parmesan (for topping)

Preheat oven to 375°F. In a food processor, purée the tofu, Nayonnaise, garlic, lemon juice, vinegar, sea salt and black pepper until well blended (scraping down the sides a couple of times). Add the artichoke hearts, spinach, parsley, and 2½ tbsp soy/rice parmesan, and pulse through until mixture starts to smooth out but still has some texture. Transfer the mixture to a small baking dish and sprinkle with the ½ tbsp soy/rice parmesan. Bake for 20-25 minutes (the top should be golden in spots). Remove, let cool slightly, and serve. This dip can be made ahead and refrigerated until ready to bake and serve, but after refrigeration, the baking time will be a little longer.

Makes roughly 2½ cups.

♥ For ⅙ of dip (roughly ½ cup, not including bread or other accompaniments): Calories: 68; Total Fat: 3.2 g (Sat. Fat: 0.4 g); Cholesterol: 0 g; Carbohydrate: 6.1 g; Fiber: 1.6 g; Protein: 4 g.

If you don't have fresh spinach on hand, you can make this dip without it - it will still taste wonderful.

Serving suggestions: Serve with "Pita/ Tortilla Crisps" (p. 68), warmed crusty bread, warmed pita bread, and/or fresh veggie nibblers. Make "Artichoke Puffs" as described on the next page, to be served as an appetizer, or as part of an entrée.

Artichoke Puffs

7-8 sheets	*phyllo pastry*
2-3 tbsp	*olive oil (or more if needed, for brushing the sheets)*
1 batch	*"Artichoke Delight Dip" (p. 58)*
½-1 tsp	*dried dill for garnish (optional)*

Preheat oven to 375°F. Take 1 phyllo sheet and brush lightly with olive oil. With a sharp knife, cut 4 strips, roughly even in width, down the length of the phyllo (1). Place a tablespoon of dip at one end of the strip, about 1 inch from corner (2). Take that corner and lift, folding filling and phyllo over (2) to form a right triangle (3). Continue to fold the triangle back and forth (3) forming triangles, until the end of the sheet, and you have a small triangular filled pastry (4). Continue this process until you have used up all the artichoke dip. Place the pastries on a baking sheet lined with parchment paper (or lightly oiled), brush tops with a little olive oil, sprinkle on the dill, and bake for 14-17 minutes, until golden. If using two baking sheets on two racks, rotate them halfway through baking, and increase the baking time to around 17-20 minutes. Remove, cool slightly, and serve warm.

Depending on how much filling you use, makes between 20-28 puffs (see sidebar).

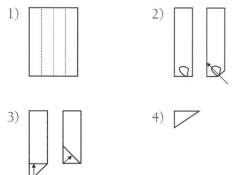

To keep the phyllo from drying out as you work, place a damp (not wet) dish towel over the stack.

Using a rounded tablespoon should yield a higher number, an even larger spoonful (about 2 tablespoons) will yield fewer triangles, about 19 or 20. Note that if you use too much dip, the triangles may "pop" somewhat while baking. which may affect their appearance.

♥ For 1 artichoke puff (based on yield of 24 pieces): Calories: 57; Total Fat: 2.7 g (Sat. Fat: 0.3 g); Cholesterol: 0; Carbohydrate: 6.5 g; Fiber: 0.6 g; Protein:1.6 g.

Best Bruschetta

	Crusty bread, cut into thin rounds or long thin slices
1½ cups	tomatoes, seeded and chopped
1 tbsp	shallots, finely minced (or ½ cup green onions, finely sliced)
¼ cup	fresh parsley, chopped
⅛ cup	black or kalamata olives, or combination, chopped (optional)
1 tbsp	olive oil
¾-1 tsp	dried oregano (see sidebar)
1	small garlic clove, finely minced (see sidebar)
¼ tsp	sea salt (see sidebar)
1 tsp	balsamic vinegar (see sidebar)
	fresh ground black pepper to taste
	soy/rice parmesan (garnish) (optional)

Preheat oven to 400°F. Place bread on a baking sheet. (If the bread is very soft or is thawing, place in oven for 5-6 minutes until just a little crusty; otherwise, your bread may be a bit soggy.) Mix topping ingredients together in a medium bowl (see sidebar on preparing ahead). If using the roasted garlic, squeeze the cloves out and mash a little, so it can be evenly distributed throughout the mixture. Place spoonfuls of the mixture onto the bread, adjusting the amount based on your preference, and how many people you are serving. If desired, sprinkle the topped breads with some soy or rice parmesan. Bake for 9-11 minutes.

Serves 6 or more.

♥ For ⅙ of the bruschetta topping, (bread not included): Calories: 37; Fat: 2.7 g (Sat. Fat: 0.3 g; Cholesterol: 0 mg; Carbohydrate: 2.9 g; Fiber: 0.7 g; Protein: 0.4 g.

You can use fresh oregano, 2-3 teaspoons chopped or more. Or, fresh basil can be used.

A wonderful option is ½-1 whole bulb of roasted garlic (for tips on roasting garlic, see p. 33). Roasted garlic gives a deeper taste and helps bind the mixture.

If preparing ahead, do not add the salt and balsamic vinegar until just before spooning the mixture on the bread to bake it. If the mixture sits with the salt and vinegar, some of the juices will be drawn out of the tomatoes.

Divine Tofu Spread or Dip

¾ cup	extra-firm tofu, squeezed dry and cubed or chopped
1	whole bulb roasted garlic (for tips on roasting garlic, see p. 33)
¼ cup	plain soy milk
¼ cup	fresh parsley, packed
2 tsp	tahini
1 tbsp	balsamic vinegar
1 tbsp	tamari (or soy sauce)
1½ tsp	mild Dijon mustard
⅛ tsp	honey option (for notes on honey options, see p. 29)
⅛ tsp	chili powder
	couple pinches sea salt
	fresh ground black pepper to taste
2 tbs	sun-dried tomatoes, chopped (see sidebar)

In a food processor, purée the tofu until it is very fine. Squeeze the roasted garlic from its bulb and add along with the remaining ingredients (except the sun-dried tomatoes) to the tofu, and purée again until very, very smooth, scraping down the sides of the processor a few times. Add the sun-dried tomatoes last, and blend until the color is imparted in the mixture, but there are still some chunky pieces. Enjoy this dip/spread as is, at room temperature, or transfer to a small baking dish and bake at 375°F for 10-13 minutes, until lightly browned on the top.
Makes roughly 1½ cups.

♥ For ⅙ of dip (roughly ¼ cup, does not include bread or other accompaniments): Calories: 63; Total Fat: 2.9 g (Sat. Fat: 0.4 g); Cholesterol: 0 mg; Carbohydrate: 5.1 g; Fiber: 0.6 g; Protein: 4.2 g.

If you don't have sun-dried tomatoes handy, use a tablespoon of tomato paste instead.

Serving suggestions: This makes an excellent dip for fresh vegetables, tortilla chips, warmed pita or crusty breads, cut into small pieces. It is also excellent as a spread on sandwiches or as a condiment for your favorite veggie burger.

Hot Nacho Dip

1 pkg	*tofu or rice "cheddar cheese," cubed (227 g, roughly 1½ cups)*
½ cup	*plain soy milk*
½-¾ cup	*salsa*
¼ cup	*spaghetti sauce*
¼ cup	*green onions, chopped*
	sea salt to taste
	fresh ground black pepper to taste

In saucepan over medium heat, add all the ingredients except the green onions. Stir the mixture fairly continuously until smooth (the mixture will blend well when it gets very hot). Once it is quite smooth, add the green onions and stir for a minute or two. If desired, season further with sea salt and fresh ground black pepper. Serve hot with nacho chips, or with "Pita/Tortilla Crisps" (p. 68). Leftover dip can be refrigerated and reheated in a saucepan. *Makes roughly 2½ cups.*

♥ For ¹⁄₁₀ of dip (roughly ¼ cup): Calories: 83; Total Fat: 4.9 g (Sat. Fat: 0.8 g); Cholesterol: 0 mg; Carbohydrate: 4.5 g; Fiber: 0.7 g; Protein: 5.2 g.

Served with nacho chips, this is a fun snack to enjoy when kicking back and watching TV. Kids will love it too, on vegetables or grains (although for kids, you may want to reduce the amount of salsa, or use a very mild one).

Mexican Tortilla Triangles

This delicious appetizer is prepared by first making a slightly spicy, very flavorful squash purée which is then spread on tortilla triangles, sprinkled with a little cornmeal, and baked until golden. The squash purée can also be served as a dip on its own, or as a spread in sandwiches, tortilla wraps, or to mix with rice or another grain.

♦

To bake the squash, clean the outside and place on upper rack of oven, with some aluminum foil or baking dish on the lower rack to catch drippings. Bake at 400°F for 40-50 minutes, or until tender when pierced with a skewer. Remove from oven, let cool until easy to handle, open and remove seeds. Scoop the flesh out. One 2½ lb squash will yield about 2½ -3 cups of cooked squash.

♦

For even more delicious triangles, top each one with caramelized onions before sprinkling with cornmeal. Quarter and slice a large onion. In a skillet, sauté in olive oil over medium heat, seasoning with sea salt and fresh ground black pepper until very soft and golden. Add a teaspoon or two of tamari or soy sauce to intensify the flavors, and deepen the color.

3	large flour tortillas (preferably sun-dried tomato flavor)
1½ cups	butternut or buttercup squash, cooked (see sidebar)
1	medium-large garlic clove, quartered
¼ cup	fresh parsley, packed
3 tbsp	sun-dried red peppers or tomatoes, reconstituted, roughly chopped
2½-3 tbsp	Nayonnaise (or other creamy, not too tangy, vegan mayonnaise)
1½-2 tbsp	cornmeal (plus a little extra to sprinkle for topping)
1½ tbsp	seasoned rice vinegar
¾ tsp	cumin
½ tsp	chili powder
½ tsp	ground coriander
¼ tsp	sea salt
	fresh ground black pepper to taste

Preheat oven to 375°F. First, make the tortilla triangles by cutting each flour tortilla into 6 or 8 triangular wedges. Place the wedges on a baking sheet lined with parchment paper (or lightly oiled). Bake for 6-8 minutes, until they start to get crispy. Remove from oven and let cool while preparing the squash purée. In a food processor, purée the squash with the garlic until very smooth. Add the remaining ingredients and purée until fairly smooth, scraping down the sides of the processor a couple of times (the red peppers can be left as small pieces throughout). Using a knife or spatula, smooth a generous layer of the squash mixture over each tortilla triangle and place back on baking sheet. Sprinkle a light layer of extra cornmeal over the triangles. Bake for 10-12 minutes at 375°F until they begin to turn golden and the tortilla shells are light brown and crispy around the edges. Serve immediately.

Makes 6-8 or more servings.

♥ With yield of 24 triangles (3 shells divided into 8 triangles each), per triangle: Calories: 38; Total Fat: 1 g (Sat. Fat: 0.2 g); Cholesterol: 0 mg; Carbohydrate: 6.1 g; Fiber: 0.7 g; Protein: 1 g.

Roasted Eggplant Dip

1	*medium eggplant (about 1 lb)*
⅓ cup	*fresh parsley, packed, chopped*
2½-3 tbsp	*tahini*
2 tbsp	*rice vinegar (preferably seasoned)*
1	*small garlic clove, roughly chopped*
½-1 tsp	*curry powder*
¼ tsp	*coriander powder*
½-1 tbsp	*olive oil*
¼ tsp	*honey option (for notes on honey options, see p. 29)*
⅛-¼ tsp	*sea salt to taste*
	fresh ground black pepper to taste

Preheat oven to 400°F. Place whole eggplant on baking dish and bake for 40-50 minutes until it is soft and collapsed a little. Remove and let cool enough to handle (it will collapse even more as it is cooling). Cut open, remove large clumps of seeds, and scoop out the flesh. Transfer flesh to a food processor and blend with all of the ingredients. Serve warm in a bowl or, as I prefer, transfer the mixture to a small baking dish and bake at 375°F for 15-20 minutes, until golden brown on top.

Makes roughly 1½ cups.

♥ For ⅙ of dip (roughly ¼ cup): Calories: 98; Total Fat: 6.4 g (Sat. Fat: 0.9 g); Cholesterol: 0 mg; Carbohydrate: 7.7 g; Fiber: 2.5 g; Protein: 2.3 g.

You can serve this dip with veggies, chips, bread, or crackers, but it is especially delicious with pappadums, the thin, light, lentil-based Indian "crackers" available in Indian markets or the imported/ethnic foods section of most grocery stores. They are very easy to prepare and complement the flavors of this dip wonderfully.

If you want to add a little extra color, try a few pinches of turmeric.

Roasted Red Pepper Dip

2	large red peppers (or 3 medium), roasted, skins removed (roughly 1-1¼ cups) (for tips on roasting peppers, see p. 33)
1	small to medium garlic clove, roughly chopped
¼ tsp	dried oregano
½ tsp	sea salt
	fresh ground black pepper to taste
½ cup	all-purpose potatoes, cubed, cooked, skins removed
1 tbsp	olive oil
¾-1 tbsp	balsamic vinegar
1 tbsp	seasoned rice vinegar
¼ cup	fresh basil, chopped

Serving Suggestions:
Serve with
"Pita/Tortilla Crisps"
(p. 68), "Parmesan
Toasts" (p. 67),
"Flatbread" (p. 67),
fresh veggies, or any
good crusty bread,
warmed and broken
into appetizer portions.

In a food processor, purée the roasted peppers with the garlic, oregano, salt, and pepper until fairly smooth. In a separate bowl, mash the potatoes with olive oil and vinegars until smooth. By hand, mix the red pepper purée into the mashed potatoes, stir in the basil, and combine until you have a smooth, consistent texture. (Do not try to purée the potatoes in the food processor, since it can activate the starches and make your potatoes gummy. If you want to add the mashed potatoes to the red pepper purée in the processor, just pulse in a couple of times, do not purée through.) Place in a baking or serving dish. Serve the dip as is at room temperature, or bake at 375°F for 17-20 minutes until it is lightly brown on top and bubbling around the edges.
Makes 1¼-1½ cups.

♥ For ⅓ of dip (roughly ¼ cup): Calories: 62; Total Fat: 2.8 g (Sat. Fat: 0.4 g); Cholesterol: 0 mg; Carbohydrate: 8.2 g; Fiber: 1.7 g; Protein: 1 g.

Super Stuffed Mushrooms

14-16	large button mushrooms, stems trimmed and reserved
½ cup	good quality breadcrumbs (reserve 1 tbsp for topping)
⅛ cup	fresh parsley, chopped
⅛ cup	celery, finely chopped
1½-2 tbsp	soy parmesan
1 tbsp	tomato paste
2 tsp	balsamic vinegar
1	small garlic clove, finely minced
½ tsp	tamari or soy sauce
½ tsp	dried mustard
½ tsp	dried oregano
¼ tsp	chili powder
	sea salt to taste
	fresh ground black pepper to taste

Preheat oven to 400°F. Remove stems from mushrooms and reserve. Place mushrooms caps with hole side up on a baking sheet lined with parchment paper. Bake for 8-9 minutes until the caps have collected some juice from the mushrooms. Remove and let cool a little. Soak up the juices with a cloth or paper towel, or tip the caps upside down, discarding the juices. For the filling, mince the mushroom stems and combine in a bowl with all the remaining ingredients (except the reserved breadcrumbs for the topping). Work the mixture until it starts to come together, binding a little when pressed. For a tighter mixture, add a little more tomato paste. Spoon filling into mushroom caps. Sprinkle on the reserved breadcrumbs and, if you wish, a little extra soy parmesan, pressing it lightly onto the stuffing. Bake at 400°F degrees for 10-12 minutes until lightly browned.
Makes 5-6 or more servings.

♥ Per mushroom (using 16 mushrooms): Calories: 16; Total Fat: 0.3 g (Sat. Fat: 0 g); Cholesterol: 0 mg; Carbohydrate: 2.2 g; Fiber: 0.4 g; Protein: 1.2 g.

Quick Side Breads and Crisps

I often make quick snacking breads and crisps to serve with meals or appetizer dips. Here are some to try:

FLATBREADS: Purchase a ready-made dough that can be rolled out (may be labeled as a pizza dough) to make a flatbread. Roll or stretch the dough out onto a lightly oiled baking sheet. The dough will thin out significantly, but does not need to spread out over the entire baking sheet. Keep the thickness fairly even, because once it bakes the thin sections will cook very quickly. Brush or spritz on a little olive oil, sprinkle with sea salt and fresh ground black pepper (and if you like, any of your favorite spices, such as chili powder, cayenne, or cumin). Bake for 10-12 minutes at 400°F, until lightly browned in spots and around the edges. Keep an eye on the bread; in the last couple of minutes it can burn quickly in the thinner spots. Remove from oven and let cool for a couple of minutes, then tear into pieces, or leave it in the pan for people to tear away pieces as they like. To jazz it up, press some of the following toppings into the stretched dough:

- fresh chopped herbs, such as thyme, rosemary, or oregano
- chopped black or kalamata olives
- chopped, reconstituted sun-dried tomatoes

PARMESAN TOASTS: For a quick and tasty side bread, brush or spritz some olive oil onto slices of good quality crusty breads (seasoned breads are especially nice, such as black olive or rosemary bread), then sprinkle on sea salt, fresh ground black pepper, and a little soy parmesan. Place the slices on a baking sheet and bake at 400°F for 9-10 minutes, until the edges are golden brown but the bread is still a little soft, not crusty throughout.

Omit the soy parmesan if you like; the breads will still be tasty. Another good idea is to use flavored olive oils, such as basil, rosemary, roasted garlic, or roasted red pepper. They not only enhance the flavoring, but some, like roasted red pepper oil, add a lovely color. Other great toppings are chopped olives and fresh chopped herbs.

PITA CRISPS/TORTILLA CRISPS: These are great with appetizer dips as well as soups. For the pita crisps, slice the pita rounds in half along the outer edge (so you have two whole rounds) then slice into one-quarter or one-sixth triangular pieces. Place on a baking sheet, spritz or brush with a little olive oil, season with sea salt, fresh ground black pepper, and any spices you like. Bake at 375° for 7-9 minutes, until they golden around the edges and a little crispy. The thinner the pita bread, the quicker it will crisp, so keep an eye on them as they cook.

For tortilla crisps, cut flour tortillas into one-sixth or one-eighth triangular pieces (flavored varieties such as spinach and sun-dried tomato are particularly nice). Place on a baking sheet, and spritz or brush with olive oil, season with sea salt, fresh ground black pepper, and any spices you like, soy parmesan if desired, and bake at 375°F for 6-7 minutes until just turning golden around the edges, but not all over. After they are removed from the oven, they will crisp more as they cool. These can burn very quickly, so watch them closely after a few minutes in the oven.

Sauces, Gravies, and Dressings

Notes for Sauces, Gravies, and Dressings

The sauce and gravy recipes here can be used to accompany different dishes, and are referenced in several recipes for serving suggestions throughout the book.

For the salad dressings, I do not use much oil, typically 2-4 tablespoons per ¾-1 cup of salad dressing. I usually add some type of natural sweetener to further cut the acidity of the vinegars and lemon juice without adding more oil. Also, I use an emulsifying agent, such as mustard or miso, so that when the oil is gradually added at the end, the dressing will thicken.

Feel free to add more oil to your dressings for more flavor and smoothness, particularly if you want to remove some of the sweeteners (the nutritional analysis averages will obviously be different). If you add extra oil, you may want to try a little flax or hemp seed oil, which I haven't included here in order to keep the number of "new" ingredients to a minimum. However, they are good substitutes for some of the olive oil, since they are rich in essential omega-3 fatty acids.

If you don't have a blender (regular or hand) to make these dressings, a covered jar works fine (except for the creamy dressings). Follow the recipes reserving the oil until last, then vigorously shake the ingredients to mix them well.

Avocado Roasted Garlic Sauce

1	*ripe avocado*
1	*whole bulb roasted garlic (for tips on roasting garlic, see p. 33)*
2-3 tsp	*lemon juice, fresh squeezed*
1 tsp	*rice vinegar (preferably seasoned)*
¼-⅓ cup	*water (or more, to desired consistency) (see sidebar)*
	sea salt to taste
	fresh ground black pepper to taste

Squeeze the roasted garlic cloves from the bulb. In a food processor or blender, combine all ingredients and blend until smooth. If sauce is too thick, add a little extra water for easy spooning. Use less water to make a dipping sauce.
Makes roughly 1 cup.

♥ For ⅙ of sauce (roughly 2-3 tbsp): Calories: 69; Total Fat: 5.1 g (Sat. Fat: 0.8 g); Cholesterol: 0 mg; Carbohydrate: 4.7 g; Fiber: 1.8 g; Protein: 1.1 g.

If you keep this sauce very thick, you can use it as a creamy dip with tortilla chips, veggies, or other munchies!

Mi-So Good Gravy!

¾ cup	water
¼ cup	brown rice miso (or another mild miso)
¼ cup	seasoned rice vinegar
1½-2 tbsp	honey option (for notes on honey options, see p. 29)
1	medium garlic clove, roughly chopped
1	tbsp arrowroot flour
1 tsp	mild Dijon mustard
½ tsp	ground ginger (or ¼ tsp fresh grated ginger)
⅛ tsp	chipotle hot sauce (or other hot sauce) (see sidebar)
	sea salt to taste
	fresh ground black pepper to taste
1½-2 tbsp	olive oil (see sidebar)

In a food processor or blender, combine all ingredients except the oil and blend. While still blending, drizzle in olive oil until well mixed. Transfer the gravy to a saucepan and heat slowly over medium heat, stirring continuously, until mixture thickens and is just about to boil. Remove from heat, season to taste with sea salt and fresh ground black pepper if desired, and serve. Or, cover the pot and reheat gently before serving. To thin out the gravy, add a tablespoon or two of water and stir.
Makes roughly 1½ cups.

♥ For ⅛ portion of gravy (roughly 3 tbsp): Calories: 72; Total Fat: 3.9 g (Sat. Fat: 0.6 g); Cholesterol: 0 mg; Carbohydrate: 8.3 g; Fiber: 0.5 g; Protein: 1 g.

This is a tangy, flavorful sauce which works well as a gravy, heated to top various potato dishes, bean and veggie patties, and grains. Experiment and enjoy!

◆

This gravy is mildly hot from the hot sauce. Adjust the amount of hot sauce depending on your taste.

◆

I have limited the oil in this gravy to keep it lower in fat. If you add another 2-3 tablespoons, the gravy will be thicker and richer in taste. So if fat content is not a big concern, the gravy will benefit from the extra oil.

◆

Serving suggestions: This gravy is wonderful with "Mushroom Pecan Burgers" (p. 114), "Lentil Miso Patties" (p. 112), including "Grate Potato Bake" (p. 128) and "Potato Chippers" (p. 149).

Mushroom Gravy

1½ tbsp	olive oil
1 cup	red or white onion, finely chopped
3-4	garlic cloves, minced
	sea salt to taste
	fresh ground black pepper to taste
2½ cups	white mushrooms, sliced
½ tsp	dried savory
½ tsp	dried oregano
¼-½ tsp	dried thyme
2 cups	vegetable stock, cool or just warm
2 tbsp	arrowroot flour
1½-2 tbsp	whole wheat pastry flour (or unbleached all-purpose flour)
1-2 tbsp	tamari or soy sauce (to taste) (see sidebar)
1-1½ tsp.	molasses

For a darker gravy, use a dark soy sauce instead of the tamari, or a little extra tamari; the gravy will darken as it reaches a boil. Keep in mind, however, that this will increase the saltiness of your gravy.

In a saucepan, heat oil over medium heat. Add onions and garlic, a pinch of sea salt and fresh ground black pepper, and sauté for 4-5 minutes, until the onions start to soften. Add mushrooms, savory, oregano, and thyme, lower the heat to medium-low, and sauté for another 4-5 minutes. Meanwhile, add a few tablespoons of vegetable stock to a small bowl. Stir arrowroot flour into the stock, blending well. Mix this back into the vegetable stock, and set aside. When mushrooms are soft, add in the whole wheat pastry flour and stir a few minutes to cook the flour. Then, stir in vegetable stock/arrowroot mixture, tamari, and molasses. Cook slowly, stirring continuously, until gravy reaches a boil and thickens, then remove from heat. Season with additional salt and pepper if desired, and serve.

Makes 5½-5¾ cups.

♥ For ⅙ of gravy (just under 1 cup): Calories: 87; Total Fat: 3.5 g (Sat. Fat: 0.5 g); Cholesterol: 0 mg; Carbohydrate: 11.3 g; Fiber: 1.2 g; Protein: 2.6 g.

Tahini-Tamari Sauce

⅓ cup + 1 tbsp tahini

⅓-½ cup water (adjust for desired thickness)

¼ cup lemon juice, fresh squeezed

¼ cup fresh parsley, chopped

2 tbsp tamari

1 tbsp rice vinegar

2 tsp honey option (2-3 tsp more if desired for a
sweeter sauce) (for notes on honey options,
see p. 29)

1 tsp toasted sesame oil

dash or two of cayenne pepper (optional)

sea salt to taste

fresh ground black pepper to taste

In a food processor or blender, combine all ingredients and blend
until smooth. Season to taste with sea salt and fresh ground black
pepper, as desired.
Makes roughly 1¼-1⅓ cups.

♥ For ¹/₁₀ of the sauce (roughly 2 tbsp): Calories: 78; Total Fat: 5.6 g
(Sat. Fat: 0.8 g); Cholesterol: 0 g; Carbohydrate: 4.7 g; Fiber: 0.6 g;
Protein: 2.2 g.

Serve over "Lightened-Up Falafels" (p. 113) or as a salad dressing or sauce as you choose!

Amazing Creamy Caesar Dressing

2	whole bulbs garlic, roasted (for tips on roasting garlic, see p. 33)
1 pkg	silken soft tofu (340 g, roughly 1¼ cups) (or regular soft tofu if necessary)
3 tbsp	lemon juice, fresh squeezed
3 tbsp	rice vinegar (or half and half seasoned rice vinegar and plain rice vinegar)
3 tbsp	Nayonnaise (or other creamy, not too tangy, vegan mayonnaise)
1½-2 tbsp	soy/rice parmesan
2 tsp	mild Dijon mustard
½ tsp	sea salt
	fresh ground black pepper to taste
	couple dashes of liquid smoke (optional)
	extra soy/rice parmesan (garnish) (optional)

Squeeze roasted garlic cloves from bulbs into a food processor. Add remaining ingredients and purée until very smooth, stopping the processor to scrape down the bowl once or twice. For a thinner dressing, purée in a little plain soy milk. Once smooth, toss the amount of dressing you want with romaine lettuce and croutons (sliced fresh mushrooms are also great). It will keep in a tight container refrigerated for 4-5 days. It will thicken once refrigerated, so thin out by stirring in a little plain soy milk. *Makes 1¾-2 cups, enough dressing for 3-4 large salads to be divided among 2-4 people.*

♥ For ⅓ of dressing (between ½ and ¾ cup): Calories: 166; Total Fat: 7 g (Sat. Fat: 0.9 g); Cholesterol: 0 mg; Carbohydrate: 16.1 g; Fiber: 0.8 g; Protein: 9.6 g.

This dressing is delicious, and because the garlic is roasted, it adds a lot of body without the need for oil! Because roasted garlic is sweet and mild compared to raw garlic, it may be preferable for many. If you like raw garlic, add half a clove for an added kick!

To make your own croutons, slice some good quality bread (multigrain or specialty flavored breads are nice) into ½ inch cubes. Spread on a baking tray, toss with a little olive oil, and sprinkle with sea salt, black pepper, and other seasonings if you like. Bake at 400°F for about 10-15 minutes until golden. Watch carefully, as they turn from golden to burned quickly! Let cool for about 10 minutes before using.

Basic Balsamic Vinaigrette

⅓ cup	balsamic vinegar
¼ - ⅓ cup	honey option (for notes on honey options, see p. 29)
1 tsp	mild Dijon mustard
2 tsp	tamari or soy sauce
½ tsp	sea salt
⅛ - ¼ tsp	fresh ground black pepper
½ tsp	dried oregano and/or rosemary (optional; crush between fingers a little) (see sidebar)
¼ cup	olive oil

In a food processor or blender, combine all ingredients except olive oil and purée. Once mixed well, continue to purée and drizzle in olive oil slowly. When finished blending, season further with sea salt and fresh ground black pepper, if desired.

Makes roughly 1 cup.

♥ For ⅛ of vinaigrette (roughly 2 tbsp): Calories: 114; Total Fat: 6.8 g (Sat. Fat: 0.9 g); Cholesterol: 0 mg; Carbohydrate: 13.1 g; Fiber: 0 g; Protein: 0.2 g.

This is a nice basic balsamic dressing that you can adjust with seasonings, and extra oil, if you wish. This can also be used as a marinade for tofu or veggies for grilling - just add a little more oil to keep veggies moist while grilling!

Substitution Ideas: You can substitute the dried herbs with others, such as basil or thyme. Add a little fresh minced ginger and/or garlic for deeper flavors.

Creamy Dijon Dill Dressing

This is one of my favorite dressings. The taste of dill and Dijon mustard together is wonderful, and the dressing itself is so rich and creamy. Good as a topping on baked potatoes, "Phyllo Spinach Pie" (p. 132), and "Grate Potato Bake" (p. 128), and goes well with tomato-based meals.

◆

By omitting the soy milk, the thickness of this dressing lends itself well as a condiment for sandwiches, veggie burgers, or as a veggie dip!

◆

Substitution Note: Although fresh dill is the "star" of this recipe, fresh basil also works wonderfully. A couple tablespoons of chopped parsley are helpful to add along with the basil, to preserve the green color.

½ cup	soft tofu, packed
¼ cup	fresh dill, roughly chopped (see sidebar)
2 tsp	mild Dijon mustard
1 tbsp	lemon juice, fresh squeezed
1 tbsp	rice vinegar (preferably seasoned)
1	small garlic clove, roughly chopped
¼-½ tsp	sea salt
	fresh ground black pepper to taste
2-3 tbsp	plain soy milk (see sidebar)
½-1 tbsp	olive oil (optional)

In a food processor or blender, combine all ingredients except olive oil and purée. Once mixed well, continue to purée and drizzle in the olive oil slowly. When finished blending, season further with sea salt and fresh ground black pepper, if desired. *Makes roughly 1 cup.*

♥ For ⅛ of dressing (roughly 2 tbsp): Calories: 29; Total Fat: 2.3 g (Sat. Fat: 0.3 g); Cholesterol: 0 mg; Carbohydrate: 0.8 g; Fiber: 0.1 g; Protein: 1.1 g.

Lemon Curry Vinaigrette

3 tbsp	*lemon juice (preferably freshly squeezed)*
2 tbsp	*orange juice (good quality or fresh squeezed)*
2 tbsp	*rice vinegar (preferably seasoned)*
¼ cup	*honey option (for notes on honey options, see p. 29) (adjust amount to taste)*
1 tsp	*mild curry paste*
2-3 tbsp	*parsley, coarsely chopped*
½ tsp	*sea salt*
	fresh ground black pepper to taste
3-4 tbsp	*olive oil*

In a food processor or blender, combine all ingredients except olive oil and purée. Once mixed well, continue to purée and drizzle in olive oil slowly. Add a bit more olive oil for a richer, smoother vinaigrette. When finished blending, season further with sea salt and fresh ground black pepper, if desired.

Makes roughly 1 cup.

♥ For ⅛ of dressing (roughly 2 tbsp): Calories: 104; Total Fat: 7.1 g (Sat. Fat: 0.9 g); Cholesterol: 0 mg; Carbohydrate: 10 g; Fiber: 0 g; Protein: 0 g.

Orange Ginger Miso Vinaigrette

¼ cup	orange juice (good quality or fresh squeezed)
2 tbsp	seasoned rice vinegar
2-2½ tbsp	honey option (for notes on honey options, see p. 29)
1 tbsp	miso (I use brown rice miso)
1 tsp	dry ginger
1 tsp	hoisin sauce
1 tsp	mild Dijon mustard
	pinch of sea salt
	fresh ground black pepper to taste
2-2½ tbsp	olive oil
2 tsp	toasted sesame oil

In a food processor or blender, combine all ingredients except olive and sesame oil and purée. Once mixed well, continue to purée and drizzle in olive and sesame oils slowly. Add a bit more olive oil for a richer, smoother vinaigrette. When finished blending, season further with sea salt and fresh ground black pepper if desired. *Makes roughly ¾ cups.*

♥ For ⅙ of dressing (roughly 2 tbsp): Calories: 109; Total Fat: 7.3 g (Sat. Fat: 1.0 g); Cholesterol: 0 mg; Carbohydrate: 10.2 g; Fiber: 0.2 g; Protein: 0.4 g.

Roasted Garlic Maple Balsamic Vinaigrette

¼ cup	*balsamic vinegar*
1	*whole bulb roasted garlic (for tips on roasting garlic, see p. 33)*
¼ cup	*orange juice (good quality or fresh squeezed)*
⅛ cup	*pure maple syrup*
1 tsp	*tamari or soy sauce*
½ tsp	*sea salt*
	fresh ground black pepper to taste
2¼ tbsp	*olive oil*

Squeeze the roasted garlic cloves out of the bulb. In a food processor or blender, combine all ingredients except olive oil and purée. Once mixed well, continue to purée and drizzle in olive oil slowly. Add a bit more olive oil for a richer, smoother vinaigrette. When finished blending, season further with sea salt and fresh ground black pepper if desired.
Makes roughly ¾ cup.

♥ For ⅙ of dressing (roughly 2 tbsp): Calories: 99; Total Fat: 6.8 g (Sat. Fat: 0.9 g); Cholesterol: 0 mg; Carbohydrate: 8.9 g; Fiber: 0.1 g; Protein: 0.6 g.

Sesame Lemon Vinaigrette

4 tbsp	*lemon juice (preferably freshly squeezed)*
1 tbsp	*rice vinegar (preferably seasoned rice vinegar)*
1½ tbsp	*hoisin sauce*
2 tbsp	*honey option (for notes on honey options, see p. 29)*
2 tsp	*toasted sesame oil*
1 tsp	*tamari*
½ tsp	*fresh ginger, grated (or ¼-½ tsp dry ginger)*
¼ tsp	*lemon zest*
	couple pinches sea salt
	pinch of fresh ground black pepper
2½ tbsp	*olive oil*
2 tsp	*toasted sesame seeds (for tips on toasting seeds, see p. 36)*

In a food processor or blender, combine all ingredients except olive oil and sesame seeds and purée. Once mixed well, continue to purée and drizzle in olive oil slowly. Add a bit more olive oil for a richer, smoother vinaigrette. When finished blending, stir in toasted sesame seeds and season further with sea salt and fresh ground black pepper if desired.

Makes roughly ¾ cup.

♥ For ⅙ of dressing (roughly 2 tbsp): Calories: 108; Total Fat: 7.7 g (Sat. Fat: 1.1 g); Cholesterol: 0 mg; Carbohydrate: 9 g; Fiber: 0.3 g; Protein: 0.4 g.

Sweet Red Wine Vinaigrette

¼ cup	red wine vinegar
⅛ cup	orange juice (good quality or fresh squeezed)
⅛ cup	honey option (for notes on honey options, see p. 29)
½ tsp	ground coriander
¼ tsp	sea salt
	fresh ground black pepper to taste
3-4 tbsp	olive oil

In a food processor or blender, combine all ingredients except olive oil and purée. Once mixed well, continue to purée and drizzle in olive oil slowly. Add a bit more olive oil for a richer, smoother vinaigrette. When finished blending, season further with sea salt and fresh ground black pepper if desired.

Makes roughly ¾ cup.

♥ For ⅙ of dressing (roughly 2 tbsp): Calories: 107; Total Fat: 9 g (Sat. Fat: 1.2 g); Cholesterol: 0 mg; Carbohydrate: 6.4 g; Fiber: 0 g; Protein: 0 g.

Soups
and Stews

Chickpea Mash Stew

1½ tbsp	olive oil
1½ cups	onion, chopped
1 cup	celery, chopped
1 cup	carrots, chopped
3	medium-large garlic cloves, chopped
¼ tsp	sea salt
	fresh ground black pepper to taste
1 cup	zucchini, chopped
1½ tsp	dried mustard
¾ tsp	ground dried sage
2	14-oz. cans chickpeas, rinsed and drained (roughly 3½ cups)
1	28-oz. can diced tomatoes (do not drain)
2 cups	vegetable stock
1 cup	water
½ cup	sun-dried tomatoes, chopped
1 tbsp	tamari
1	large dried bay leaf
2 tsp	molasses
1 tbsp	fresh thyme, chopped

In a large soup pot, heat olive oil over medium heat. Add onions, celery, carrots, garlic, sea salt, and black pepper. Cover and cook for 6-8 minutes until the vegetables soften (stir a couple of times throughout). Add zucchini, dried mustard, and sage, and stir for a couple of minutes. Add remaining ingredients except fresh thyme and bring to a boil. Reduce heat and let simmer covered for 15-20 minutes. Remove but reserve bay leaf, and mash or lightly purée the soup (keeping a chunky texture), then stir in fresh thyme. Add bay leaf back in and let simmer for another 3-5 minutes. Remove bay leaf before serving, and season with additional sea salt and fresh ground black pepper if desired.
Makes 6-8 servings.

♥ For 8 servings, per serving: Calories: 232; Total Fat: 5 g (Sat. Fat: 0.5 g); Cholesterol: 0 mg; Carbohydrate: 36.3 g; Fiber: 9.4 g; Protein: 10.3 g.

Puréed Curried Squash and Yam Soup

1	large butternut squash (6-7 cups cooked)
2	very large yams (3 cups cooked)
2 tsp	olive oil
1 cup	red or white onion, roughly chopped
½ cup	celery, roughly chopped
	few pinches sea salt
	few pinches fresh ground black pepper
3	medium-large garlic cloves, chopped
1 tbsp	fresh ginger, grated (or 1 tsp dry ginger)
1 tsp	curry powder
½ tsp	coriander powder
¼ tsp	cinnamon
4 cups	vegetable stock
1-1½ cups	water

Instead of 1 large squash, you could use 2 smaller ones, roughly 4½ pounds in total. Similarly, instead of 2 very large yams, you could use several average size ones, roughly 2-2½ pounds in total.

This makes a very large batch of soup, enough for several meals, and freezes well.

Preheat oven to 400°F. Bake squash and yams for 55-60 minutes, or until soft when pierced (the squash may need longer, particularly if using one large squash). Remove from oven and let cool enough to handle. Prepare other ingredients while squash and yams are baking and cooling. Once cooled, slice squash and yams and scoop flesh from peels (discard seeds and strings from the squash). In a large soup pot, heat the olive oil over medium heat. Add onion, celery, sea salt, and fresh ground black pepper. Cover and cook for a few minutes. If the mixture gets dry, add a little water or stock. Stir in garlic, ginger, curry powder, coriander, and cinnamon. Cover and cook for another 4-5 minutes, until the onions soften. Add vegetable stock, 1 cup water, and squash and yam flesh. Using a hand blender, or transferring the mixture to a food processor, purée the soup until smooth. Add extra water if desired for a thinner soup. Bring the mixture to a boil, reduce heat to low, cover, and let simmer for roughly 10 minutes. Season to taste with extra sea salt and fresh ground black pepper as desired.
Makes 8-10 servings.

♥ For 10 servings, per serving: Calories: 250; Total Fat: 2.4 g (Sat. Fat: 0.4 g); Cholesterol: 0 mg; Carbohydrate: 52.4 g; Fiber: 10.8 g; Protein: 4.6 g.

Puréed Roasted Parsnip and Fennel Soup

5-6 cups	parsnips, sliced in 1" rounds and half-rounds where very thick
2	fennel bulbs (stalks and core discarded), chopped into large pieces
½ tsp	sea salt, plus a few extra pinches to sauté
	fresh ground black pepper to taste
2-2½ tbsp	olive oil (to coat parsnip and fennel)
½-1 tbsp	olive oil (to sauté onion and celery)
1 cup	onion, chopped
½ cup	celery, chopped
1 tsp	mustard seeds
2 cups	vegetable stock
4 cups	water
1 tsp	fresh rosemary, finely chopped

Preheat oven to 400°F. In a bowl, toss the parsnip, fennel, sea salt, and a few pinches of fresh ground black pepper with the 2-2½ tbsp olive oil. Place on two baking sheets lined with parchment paper (or lightly oiled). Bake for roughly 1 hour, rotating the sheets from top to bottom halfway through and tossing once or twice throughout, until the parsnip and fennel are tender and have a light golden color. As it is finishes cooking, heat remaining ½-1 tbsp olive oil in a soup pot over medium heat, and sauté onions, celery, and mustard seeds with a pinch of sea salt and fresh ground black pepper, for 5-7 minutes, until the onion and celery have softened. If they start to dry out while cooking, add a little of the water or vegetable stock. Add the stock, water, roasted fennel and parsnip to the pot. Using a hand blender, or transferring mixture to a food processor, purée until quite smooth, or to the texture desired. Bring to a boil, then immediately reduce heat to low. Stir in rosemary, and season with sea salt and fresh ground black pepper to taste. Cover and let simmer for 5-10 minutes.
Makes 6-8 servings.

♥ For 8 servings, per serving: Calories: 193; Total Fat: 6.6 g (Sat. Fat: 0.8 g); Cholesterol: 0 mg; Carbohydrate: 29.8 g; Fiber: 9.5 g; Protein: 3.7 g.

Soul-Full Chili

2½ cups	red onion, chopped
1 tbsp	olive oil
1½ cups	celery, chopped
1 cup	carrots, finely chopped
2½-3 tbsp	garlic, minced
½ tsp	sea salt
	fresh ground black pepper to taste
1 tbsp	chili powder
1 tsp	dried oregano
¾ tsp	cumin
⅛ tsp	cinnamon
⅛ tsp	red pepper flakes (optional)
2½ cups	combination red, green, and/or yellow peppers, chopped
2 cups	frozen corn kernels (or fresh corn cut from cob)
1 cup	kidney beans, cooked
1 cup	black beans, cooked
2	28-oz cans diced tomatoes (do not drain)
1	156-ml / 5½-oz can tomato paste (preferably spicy or garlic)
½ tsp	chipotle hot sauce (or other hot sauce)
1 tbsp	dark soy sauce (or tamari)
1 tsp	unrefined sugar (or white or brown sugar)

In a large soup pot, sauté onions in olive oil over medium heat for 2-3 minutes (cover, stirring occasionally). Add celery and carrots, cook for another 2-3 minutes, then add garlic, salt and pepper, chili powder, oregano, cumin, cinnamon, and red pepper flakes. Stir and cook for 3-4 minutes. (If ingredients are dry, add a bit of water.) Add peppers and corn, and cook another 3-4 minutes (cover and stir). Add beans, diced tomatoes, tomato paste, hot sauce, soy sauce, and sugar. Turn heat to high and let the chili come to a boil. Reduce heat to low and let simmer covered for 20 minutes. Adjust seasonings with extra sea salt and fresh ground black pepper if desired.

Makes 8-10 servings.

♥ For 10 servings, per serving: Calories: 213; Total Fat: 2.7 g (Sat. Fat: 0.4 g); Cholesterol: 0 mg; Carbohydrate: 38.7 g; Fiber: 9.9 g; Protein: 8.5 g.

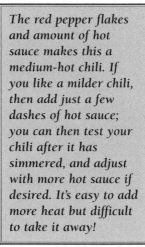

Substitution Note: Instead of corn, you can use other veggies, such as chopped zucchini or button mushrooms. Also, if you prefer another type of bean, substitute them for some or all of the kidney or black beans.

♦

The red pepper flakes and amount of hot sauce makes this a medium-hot chili. If you like a milder chili, then add just a few dashes of hot sauce; you can then test your chili after it has simmered, and adjust with more hot sauce if desired. It's easy to add more heat but difficult to take it away!

Spicy Thai Stew

1 tbsp	toasted sesame oil or olive oil
2 cups	onion, chopped
2 cups	yams, chopped
1 cup	carrots, diced
	sea salt to taste
	fresh ground black pepper to taste
1 cup	celery, chopped
4-5	garlic cloves, pressed or minced
¼ -½ tsp	red chili pepper, finely chopped
1 tsp	ground coriander
2 cups	red pepper, chopped
1½ tbsp	fresh ginger, grated
2 cups	vegetable stock
2 cups	water
⅓ cup	almond butter (or more, to taste) (other nut butters can be used)
3 tbsp	tamari
2½ tbsp	balsamic vinegar
1 tsp	molasses
3½-4 cups	Swiss chard, packed, chopped large
3-4 tbsp	fresh cilantro, chopped (or parsley)
1 tsp	toasted sesame oil (optional, for finishing)

This stew is quite hearty, with a lot of chunky vegetables. If you want soup with more broth, simply add a little extra water and/or vegetable stock. You may also want to adjust your seasonings to taste.

Substitution note: Add more chili pepper for a hotter stew. Or try different varieties of hot peppers, again adjusting the amount to your preference (and tolerance) for heat! Dried red chili flakes can also be used instead of fresh peppers; use about ¼ teaspoon, or more if you like. Also, instead of Swiss chard, you could also use fresh spinach leaves or bok choy leaves.

In a soup pot, heat the 1 tbsp sesame or olive oil over medium heat. Add onions, yams, carrots, a couple pinches sea salt and fresh ground black pepper. Cover and cook for 4-5 minutes, stirring a few times. Add the celery, garlic, chili pepper, ground coriander, another dash of sea salt, and cover again to cook for another 2-3 minutes. Add red pepper and ginger, stir for a minute, then add vegetable stock, water, almond butter, tamari, balsamic vinegar, and molasses. Bring the stew to a boil, then reduce heat to low and let simmer for 13-15 minutes, stirring a couple of times throughout. If carrots and yams are not tender, cover the pot and simmer for another few minutes. Once vegetables are tender, stir in Swiss chard, cilantro, and remaining sesame oil. Stir for a minute or two until Swiss chard leaves have just wilted but are still a nice green color. Season further with additional sea salt and fresh ground black pepper if desired.

(Note: Do not add the Swiss chard and cilantro until just before you are ready to serve. If making ahead of time, reheat 4-5 minutes prior to serving, add in Swiss chard and cilantro, and stir through until just wilted. Otherwise they will lose their vibrancy in taste and color if left in the pot to simmer for too long.)
Makes 6-8 servings.

♥ For 8 servings, per serving: Calories: 195; Total Fat: 8.8 g (Sat. Fat: 0.9 g); Cholesterol: 0 mg; Carbohydrate: 24.3 g; Fiber: 4.5 g; Protein: 4.9 g.

A wonderful addition to this stew is to top individual servings with "Tasty Tofu Tidbits" (p. 158).

Velvety Roasted Herbed Tomato Soup

3½-4 lbs	ripe tomatoes (preferably Roma)
10-12	medium-large garlic cloves, halved or quartered
1½ tbsp	olive oil (to brush tomatoes)
2 tbsp	balsamic vinegar
1 tbsp	dark soy sauce or tamari
2 tsp	dried oregano
2 tsp	dried basil
½ tsp	sea salt
¼ tsp	fresh ground black pepper
½ tbsp	olive oil (to sauté onions)
1 cup	onions, chopped
2 cups	vegetable stock
2 cups	water
½ tsp	unrefined sugar (or white sugar)
¼ cup	fresh basil, chopped
2 tbsp	fresh oregano or thyme, finely chopped

Preheat oven to 400°F. Line a large, rimmed (to catch juices) baking sheet (or two smaller ones) with parchment paper. Cut stems from tomatoes, and slice each into halves (if tomatoes are large, cut them into thirds). Place tomatoes, cut side up, on baking sheets. Insert cut cloves of garlic into the seedy portions of some of the tomatoes, to keep them moist while roasting. Brush the tomatoes with the 1½ tbsp olive oil. Combine balsamic vinegar and soy sauce with dried oregano and basil, and brush or spread over tomatoes. Sprinkle tomatoes with sea salt and black pepper, place the baking sheets in the oven, and roast for roughly 75-80 minutes until they are very soft and a little blackened around the edges. If using two baking sheets, rotate the sheets once halfway through the roasting time.

This is a light soup, so if this is a main course, serve with a hearty bread and a mixed salad. For a heartier soup, you could serve this on top of cooked rice, along with a salad and "Flatbread" (p. 67). Also, try tossing leftover soup with some cooked beans and pasta for a quick and satisfying meal.

As tomatoes are finishing, heat the ½ tbsp olive oil in a soup pot over medium heat. Add onions and a dash of sea salt and black pepper, and cook covered for 5-7 minutes, until softened, stirring occasionally. Add roasted tomatoes and garlic to the soup pot, scraping any juices and herbs from baking sheets into the pot. Add stock, water, and sugar, and stir. Using a hand blender, or transferring the mixture to a food processor, purée until smooth. Bring the mixture to a boil, then reduce heat to low. Add fresh basil and oregano, cover and let simmer for a few minutes before serving. (If not serving right away, do not add the fresh herbs until 5-10 minutes before serving.) Season with additional sea salt and fresh ground black pepper if desired.

Makes 6 or more servings.

♥ For 6 servings, per serving: Calories: 151; Total Fat: 5.6 g (Sat. Fat: 0.7 g); Cholesterol: 0 mg; Carbohydrate: 21.2 g; Fiber: 4.5 g; Protein: 4.3 g.

Wild Rice and Mushroom Stew

This is a savory, rich, earthy soup that is wonderfully comforting. This recipe makes a huge batch of soup, enough for a couple of meals and another batch to freeze!

1½ tbsp	olive oil
2 cups	red onion, chopped
	sea salt to taste
	fresh ground black pepper to taste
4-5	garlic cloves, minced
10-11 cups	fresh mushrooms, thickly sliced (roughly 2-2½ lbs.)
1 cup	dried wild rice (or other rice, if you prefer)
5 cups	water
2 cups	vegetable stock
⅛-¼ cup	tamari (adjust to taste, depending on saltiness of stock)
3 tbsp	hoisin sauce

2 tsp	*dried oregano (or 2 tbsp fresh oregano, chopped)*
1-2 tsp	*dried thyme (or 1½-2 tbsp fresh thyme, chopped)*
1	*large dried bay leaf (or 2 small)*
2-3 tbsp	*arrowroot flour, mixed with a few tablespoons of water (optional)*
	fresh parsley, minced (garnish) (optional)
	toasted pecans, chopped (garnish – for tips on toasting nuts, see p. 36) (optional)

In a large soup pot, heat olive oil over medium heat. Add chopped onions and a dash of salt and pepper and sauté for 2-3 minutes. Add garlic and continue to sauté for another 1-2 minutes, until the onions soften, then add sliced mushrooms and another dash of salt. Cover and let cook, occasionally tossing mushrooms gently, for 6-7 minutes, until they start to wilt. Stir in rice, water, vegetable stock, and remaining ingredients (except optional arrowroot and fresh herbs) and stir. (If using fresh herbs instead of dried, add them during last minutes of cooking so that they do not overcook and lose their wonderful flavors). Turn heat up to high and bring soup to a boil. Reduce heat to low, then cover and let simmer for 60-70 minutes, or until wild rice is completely cooked and has opened to expose the inner white part of the grain (if you use another rice, you will not need to cook as long). To thicken the stew a little, add the optional arrowroot mixture, bring to a boil, then immediately reduce the heat again. Season with additional sea salt and black pepper if desired. Remove bay leaf, pour into individual bowls, and garnish with a sprinkling of parsley and toasted pecans.

Makes 8-10 servings.

♥ For 10 servings, per serving: Calories: 156; Total Fat: 3 g (Sat. Fat: 0.4 g); Cholesterol: 0 mg; Carbohydrate: 26 g; Fiber: 3.5 g; Protein: 6.7 g.

> *The combination of mushrooms is up to you! I like to use about 4-5 cups of button mushrooms, 3-4 cups of portabella, and shiitake, oyster, or chanterelle for the remainder. Adding just a few cups of wild mushrooms will enhance the flavors!*

> *Serve with a fresh green salad and crusty bread. You could also serve it on top of mashed potatoes (mashed with a little olive oil, plain soy milk, salt and pepper; roasted garlic would also be nice).*

Salads and Sandwiches

Cool Cucumber Tomato Toss

1 cup	cucumber, seeded and chopped into small chunks
1 cup	tomatoes, seeded and chopped into small chunks
1 cup	jicama, chopped into small chunks (thick skin removed) (see sidebar)
2 tsp	fresh lime juice (or lemon juice)
1 tbsp	balsamic vinegar
1 tbsp	olive oil
2-3 tbsp	fresh cilantro or basil, chopped
2-3 tbsp	fresh parsley, chopped
½ tsp	honey option (for notes on honey options, see p. 29)
⅛ tsp	ground coriander
	sea salt to taste
	fresh ground black pepper to taste

In a medium to large bowl, toss all of the ingredients together until well combined and serve immediately. (If not serving immediately, reserve the jicama, lime or lemon juice, balsamic vinegar, and sea salt. Toss the jicama with a little of the lime juice and set aside. Then, just before serving, toss the jicama along with the remaining lime or lemon juice, balsamic vinegar, and sea salt into the premixed ingredients.)

Makes 3-4 servings.

♥ For 4 servings, per serving: Calories: 61; Total Fat: 3.5 g (Sat. Fat: 0.5 g); Cholesterol: 0 mg; Carbohydrate: 6.7 g; Fiber: 2.3 g; Protein: 0.8 g.

Jicama is a vegetable which resembles a turnip in shape, but is beige in color. Its taste is like a cross between apple and cucumber, and its texture is similar to a water chestnut. To eat it, remove the skin and about ½ inch of flesh beneath the skin. The flesh is crunchy, a little juicy, and just a bit sweet. It is available in most grocery stores. If jicama is unavailable, substitute some celery and a little more cucumber in its place.

A really great olive oil, or a flavored olive oil (such as basil), will work wonderfully in this recipe.

Roasted Potato Salad

2 lbs	red or Yukon Gold potatoes, cut in small cubes (about 1" width) (roughly 5 cups)
2 tsp	olive oil (for potatoes)
¼ tsp	sea salt
	few pinches fresh ground black pepper
1	170-ml jar artichoke hearts, drained, rinsed, and chopped (½ cup)
⅓-½ cup	sun-dried red peppers (or tomatoes), reconstituted and chopped
2-2½ tbsp	fresh dill or basil (or combination), chopped
3-4 tsp	olive oil (a flavored olive oil is especially nice, such as basil)
1 tsp	balsamic vinegar
2 tsp	soy/rice parmesan (optional)

This is a wonderful light alternative to potato salads that are heavy on mayonnaise. It has great flavors from the roasted potatoes, as well as the fresh herbs, olive oil, and artichokes. A great lunch, side dish, or light snack.

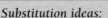

Substitution ideas:
- Instead of cubed red or Yukon gold potatoes, you could use whole baby potatoes, about 1 inch wide.
- Turn this into a pasta salad by using leftover cooked pasta instead of potatoes.
- Instead of, or in addition to fresh herbs, try some fresh chopped green onions or chives. Other additions might include chopped green bell peppers or black olives.
- For a creamy salad, omit some or all of the olive oil used for tossing the salad, and replace it with some Nayonnaise.

Preheat oven to 400°F. Toss potatoes with the 2 tsp olive oil, sea salt, and black pepper, and place on a baking sheet lined with parchment paper (or lightly oiled). Bake for 35-45 minutes, until the potatoes are tender and golden in spots. Remove from oven and let cool. In a large bowl, toss potatoes with remaining ingredients. Season with extra sea salt, fresh ground black pepper, and a little more olive oil if desired. This is best served warm or at room temperature, but can be served chilled (if refrigerating, note that the potatoes will absorb a lot of the oil, so you may want to add extra olive oil to remoisten when serving).
Makes 4-5 servings.

♥ For 5 servings, per serving: Calories: 226; Total Fat: 5.9 g (Sat. Fat: 0.7 g); Cholesterol: 0 mg; Carbohydrate: 37.8 g; Fiber: 4.5 g; Protein: 5.6 g.

Simple Salad Suggestions

Here are some nifty salad ideas (to serve roughly 4-5 people). Use any of the dressing recipes in the "Sauces, Gravies, and Salad Dressings" section (p. 69), or your own favorites!

MIXED WILD GREENS SALAD

4½-5 cups	*mixed wild greens*
1-1½ cups	*tomatoes, sliced (Roma are nice)*
¼ cup	*fresh parsley, chopped*
	few pinches fresh ground black pepper

Place mixed wild greens in salad bowl. Arrange sliced tomatoes on top. Sprinkle with fresh parsley, and season with fresh ground black pepper. Add dressing of your choice and toss well.

SPINACH SALAD

4½-5 cups	*fresh spinach, torn into pieces*
1	*yellow pepper, cored, halved, and thinly sliced*
1-1½ cups	*white button mushrooms, sliced*
¼ cup	*sun-dried red peppers or tomatoes, reconstituted and chopped*
2-3 tbsp	*fresh parsley or basil, chopped*
2 tbsp	*toasted pine nuts or sliced almonds (for tips on toasting nuts, see p. 36)*
	few pinches fresh ground black pepper

Place spinach in salad bowl. Arrange yellow pepper around the edge of the spinach. Place mushrooms in the center of the salad. Sprinkle sun-dried tomatoes and nuts, and season with fresh ground black pepper. Add dressing of your choice and toss well.

GARDEN MEDLEY

4½-5 cups	red leaf, green leaf, or romaine lettuce (or combination)
½-¾ cup	carrots, finely grated
½ cup	beets, finely grated
¼-½ cup	fresh chives or green onions (green portion only), chopped
2 tbsp	toasted sesame or pumpkin seeds (for tips on toasting seeds, see p. 36)
	fresh ground black pepper

In a salad bowl, toss lettuce with carrots and beets, then sprinkle with chopped chives or green onions and toasted seeds, and season with fresh ground black pepper. Add dressing of your choice and toss well.

"ZUCCHADO" SALAD

4½-5 cups	red leaf, green leaf, or romaine lettuce (or combination)
1 cup	zucchini, grated
1	avocado, peeled and pitted, sliced in thin strips or cut into small chunks
1	red pepper, cored and thinly sliced
¼ cup	fresh parsley or cilantro, chopped
¼ cup	chives or green onion (green portion only), chopped
	fresh ground black pepper

Place lettuce in a salad bowl. Evenly sprinkle grated zucchini over top. Arrange avocado in center of salad and red pepper around the edges. Sprinkle with chopped parsley or cilantro, and chopped chives or green onions, and season with fresh ground black pepper. Add dressing of your choice and toss well.

MIXED VEG SALAD

4½-5 cups	*green leaf, red leaf, or romaine lettuce (or combination)*
¼-½ cup	*celery, thinly sliced*
½ cup	*cucumber, seeded and sliced*
¼-½ cup	*jicama, cubed, or snow peas, thinly sliced*
1	*small red or orange pepper, cored and thinly sliced*
½ cup	*veggie of choice (e.g. chopped broccoli or cauliflower)*
	fresh ground black pepper

Place lettuce in a salad bowl. Arrange celery, cucumber, and jicama or snow peas over top, and then arrange sliced peppers and your other veggie of choice around the edges. Sprinkle with parsley or cilantro and season with fresh ground black pepper. Add dressing of your choice and toss well.

◆

Try other combinations of vegetables that look wonderful and fresh at the market, especially when in season, such as chopped tomatoes, cucumbers, with chopped fresh chives or basil; julienned (chopped in long thin pieces, similar to matchsticks) carrots, red pepper, and jicama or cucumber, tossed with sunflower or sesame seeds and chopped parsley; or a simple mixture of wonderful fresh mixed greens, tossed with peppery greens such as arugula.

You can also use your favorite vegetables, seeds, and nuts in place of some of these ingredients. For example, replace sesame or pumpkin seeds with sunflower seeds, or the snow peas or peppers with finely chopped broccoli or cauliflower florets (blanch first, if you wish). Think of adding different vegetables that are in season at the time, such as some roasted or blanched asparagus, and the varieties of tomatoes that are most ripe and in season.

Egg-Less Sandwich Filling

1 cup	extra-firm tofu, squeezed dry and mashed well or minced in food processor (see tips on preparing tofu, p. 31)
1 tbsp	rice vinegar
2 tsp	mild Dijon mustard
½ cup	green pepper, finely chopped
¼ cup	celery, finely chopped
¼ cup	Nayonnaise (or other creamy, not too tangy vegan mayonnaise)
2 tbsp	fresh dill, chopped (or 1 tsp. dried)
1½-2 tbsp	chives or green onions (green part only), chopped
½ tsp	honey option (for notes on honey options, see p. 29)
¼ tsp	turmeric
⅛ tsp	sea salt
	fresh ground black pepper to taste

In a mixing bowl, combine the tofu with vinegar and mustard and mix well. Add remaining ingredients and mix until well combined. Season with additional sea salt and fresh ground black pepper if desired. Serve as you would an egg salad, as a sandwich filling, or as one of the options described in the sidebar.
Makes 4-6 servings.

♥ For 6 servings, per serving: Calories: 71; Total Fat: 4.6 g (Sat. Fat: 0.7 g); Cholesterol: 0 mg; Carbohydrate: 3.4 g; Fiber: 0.5 g; Protein: 4 g.

You could use this filling in a sandwich or in a whole wheat pita pocket with other fresh veggies, such as lettuce, tomato, and cucumber. You can also serve it on top of mixed greens and drizzle over a little balsamic vinaigrette for a nice, hearty salad. A great idea for an appetizer is to put spoonfuls inside miniature pita breads, or spread a very thin layer on a flour tortilla, roll it up, and cut into slices.

Grilled Soy Cheese Sandwiches

1½ tsp	olive oil
3-4	soy or rice cheese slices
4 slices	good quality bread
3 tbsp	green onions, chopped
2-3 tbsp	sun-dried tomatoes, reconstituted and chopped
2 tbsp	red pepper, finely chopped
	few pinches sea salt
	few pinches fresh ground black pepper

In a large skillet, heat oil over medium heat. To assemble, place 1 slice of soy/rice cheese on piece of bread. Sprinkle half of the veggie toppings over cheese slice, a pinch of sea salt and fresh ground black pepper, and then place another half rice slice, torn in pieces, over the veggies. (If using large slices of bread, you may want to use two full rice slices per sandwich.) Top with another slice of bread. Repeat steps for second sandwich, then carefully transfer both to skillet. Cover and cook for 3-5 minutes on each side (press down lightly a couple of times while cooking, to help the cheese melt on to both sides of the bread), until the cheese is melted through and the bread is turning golden. Continue to grill the sandwiches uncovered for a minute or two on each side to brown and crisp around the edges (if not already). If the bread begins to brown before the cheese has melted, turn heat down to fairly low and cover skillet until cheese melts. Conversely, if bread is not browning but cheese is melted, remove cover and turn heat up a little.

Makes 1-2 servings.

♥ For 2 sandwiches (using 3 soy/rice cheese slices), per sandwich: Calories: 244; Total Fat: 8.6 g (Sat. Fat: 0.9 g); Cholesterol: 0 mg; Carbohydrate: 29.7 g; Fiber: 4.3 g; Protein: 12.2 g.

> *Try using pita bread instead of regular bread. Fill halved pitas with the ingredients (keep the fillings about an inch from the pita opening to keep the melted cheese from oozing out).*
> *Or try grilled tortilla cheeses: put the fillings on one half of a flour tortilla, and then fold the other half over to cover (you may want to use less cheese).*

> *You can use other vegetables and seasonings instead of some of the ones listed here. Options include fresh spinach leaves, fresh chopped herbs (basil, parsley, oregano, or dill), chili powder, chopped black olives, and chopped mushrooms. Try not to use many vegetables that are very wet (such as cucumbers, or very moist tomatoes), since they interfere with the cheese melting nicely.*

Lentil Veggie Wraps

½ cup	split red lentils, cooked
½ tsp	toasted sesame oil
1½ tsp	seasoned rice vinegar
¼ tsp	ground coriander
	few pinches sea salt
	few pinches fresh ground black pepper
2-3	large flour tortillas
½ cup	carrots, finely grated
½ cup	cucumber, seeded and cut into 2" strips
¾-1 cup	red, yellow, or green pepper, finely sliced
½	medium avocado, sliced
¼ cup	fresh parsley or cilantro, finely chopped
2-4 tsp	vinaigrette (e.g., "Orange Miso" [p. 79] or "Sesame Lemon" [p. 81])

Mash lentils with sesame oil, rice vinegar, coriander, sea salt, and black pepper until you have a thick, spreadable mixture. Spread on tortilla shells, leaving about a 1" edge uncovered. In the center of each tortilla, place grated carrot in a line from one end of the tortilla to the other, again leaving about 1" at each end without the topping. Follow this pattern with cucumber, peppers, avocado, and parsley. Drizzle a little vinaigrette along the length of the veggies. To fold the wraps, take one side and bring it in over the vegetables, fold the bottom edge over this side, and then fold over the remaining side (the top end will be open). If you are not serving these right away, tightly wrap each tortilla in plastic wrap to hold it together.

♥ For 3 wraps (using chutney instead of vinaigrette), per wrap: Calories: 349; Total Fat: 10.3 g (Sat. Fat: 1.9 g); Cholesterol: 0 mg; Carbohydrate: 54.2 g; Fiber: 8.6 g; Protein: 9.7 g.

You can play with the ingredients in these wraps, and adjust how much filling you use. If you want a big wrap, use 2 large tortillas (in which case you won't use all of the lentil spread), or for thinner wraps, use 3 tortillas.

Instead of cucumber, try jicama, or a combination of both. And instead of the vinaigrette, try 2-3 tablespoons of mango chutney or another chutney.

I use split red lentils because they cook quickly and turn into a purée easily, but you can use other lentils or beans. A quick substitution is prepared hummus (you will not need the sesame oil, rice vinegar, or coriander). If you want an even heartier wrap, add cooked rice or other cooked grain to the fillings.

Marinated Tofu Sandwich Filling

1 cup	tofu, marinated, fried, and mashed (see sidebar)
1 cup	tomatoes, seeded and chopped
¾ cup	red pepper, finely chopped
¼ cup	celery, diced
¼ cup	chives or green onions, chopped
⅛-¼ cup	fresh parsley, chopped
¾-1 tsp	mild Dijon mustard
3-4 tbsp	Nayonnaise
	fresh ground black pepper to taste

In a mixing bowl, add all ingredients and combine well.
Makes 3-4 servings as a sandwich filling.

NOTE: If you don't have leftover marinated/fried tofu, prepare as follows:

1 tbsp	soy sauce
2 tsp	balsamic vinegar
	dash hot sauce (optional)
1 cup	extra-firm or firm tofu (squeezed dry and mashed well, or puréed in food processor until crumbly - see tips on preparing and marinating tofu, p. 31)
½ tbsp	olive oil

In a bowl, combine soy sauce, balsamic vinegar, and hot sauce and then add tofu, mixing well. Cover and marinate for 15-20 minutes if possible, but you can use right away. In a skillet, heat oil and fry tofu for 7-10 minutes over medium-high heat, turning the sides, until it starts to brown and sear. Let cool to prepare filling.
Makes 3-4 servings.

♥ For 4 servings (filling alone), per serving: Calories: 134; Total Fat: 8.7 g (Sat. Fat: 1.3 g); Cholesterol: 0 mg; Carbohydrate: 7.6 g; Fiber: 1.6 g; Protein: 6.6 g.

This is a great way to use leftover tofu that you have marinated and fried. If you don't have leftover tofu, then simply follow the instructions below to prepare the tofu. The filling can be used in pita pockets, on tortillas, or on your favorite bread. Also a great salad topping.

This is a very flexible recipe, and you can use other chopped vegetables in place of the red pepper or the celery, such as zucchini, cucumber, green pepper, or carrot. As well, instead of the fresh parsley, you could substitute cilantro, basil, or dill.

Main Courses

For the pasta sauces, I have not included the amount of dry or fresh pasta, as I like to serve more sauce with my pasta servings than average. In general, however, these sauces will coat enough pasta to serve 3-4 people, sometimes more, so 1 pound of dry pasta is a good amount to cook for most recipes. These sauces can also be used to top rice or other grains.

Best-o Pesto Sauce

¾ cup	soft or medium tofu, patted dry
1 tbsp	fresh lemon juice
2	whole bulbs roasted garlic (for tips on roasting garlic, see p. 33)
¼ tsp	sea salt
⅛ tsp	fresh ground black pepper
¾ cup	fresh parsley, packed
2-3 tbsp	soy/rice parmesan
4 cups	fresh basil, packed
3 tbsp	toasted pecans, pine nuts, or walnuts (optional) (for tips on toasting nuts, see p. 36)
2 tbsp	olive oil (or more, to taste, see sidebar)

Squeeze roasted garlic cloves out of bulbs. In a food processor, purée tofu with lemon juice, roasted garlic, sea salt, and black pepper. Add parsley and parmesan and purée. Add basil, optional nuts, and olive oil last, and blend until nicely puréed, scraping down the bowl sides a couple of times (do not blend too long or the basil will bruise a lot). Season with additional sea salt and black pepper if desired. Serve tossed with pasta or rice.

Store leftover pesto in a container with a tight-fitting lid for up to 3-4 days. Once stored, the top layer will discolor, but this can either be scraped off lightly, or mixed in again.
Makes roughly 2 cups.

♥ For 4 servings (roughly ½ cup), (not including pasta): Calories: 194; Total Fat: 13.2 g (Sat. Fat: 1.5 g); Cholesterol: 0 mg; Carbohydrate: 11.6 g; Fiber: 3 g; Protein: 7.5 g.

Pesto is typically made with a lot of oil, nuts, and parmesan, so it can be quite high in fat. I love a generous amount of pesto with my pasta, so I came up with this version that is reduced in fat, but not in flavor!

Adding more olive oil will certainly enrich the flavors and texture. Keep in mind, though, that this will also increase the fat content. For extra "zing," add an additional fresh garlic clove, chopped.

Try this pesto as a base for pizzas, a topping on baked potatoes, a sandwich spread, or tossed with steamed veggies or cold vegetable salads.

Basic Creamy Garlic Sauce

3	whole bulbs roasted garlic (for tips on roasting garlic, see p. 33)

½ cup	vegetable stock
2-3 cups	assorted fresh vegetables (see sidebar)
1 tbsp	olive oil (for sauté)
⅛-¼ tsp	sea salt
	fresh ground black pepper to taste
⅓ cup	white wine
⅓ cup	fresh leafy herbs (see sidebar)
2-3 tbsp	soy/rice parmesan
1 tbsp	olive oil (for finishing) (optional)

This recipe is the foundation for the next two sauce recipes. Choose your favorite vegetables to use, or omit the vegetables altogether.

♦

For the vegetables, I recommend quick-cooking ones. Try 1 cup chopped asparagus, 2 cups mushrooms, and fresh basil. Sauté the mushrooms first, then add the asparagus with the garlic purée, and the basil tossed at the end.

♦

For the herbs, use basil, cilantro, or parsley, or 1-2 tbsp of a stronger herb such as thyme or oregano. These stronger herbs can be added a little earlier, as they impart a heavier flavor, and can be cooked a little longer.

Squeeze roasted garlic cloves from bulbs into vegetable stock. Using a hand blender or in a food processor, purée the mixture and set aside. In a saucepan, sauté vegetables over medium-high heat in the 1 tbsp olive oil for 4-5 minutes, adding sea salt and black pepper. Turn heat to high and add wine. Cook for a few minutes to allow some of the liquid to evaporate, and alcohol to burn off. Once some of the liquid has evaporated, turn heat to medium-low, add puréed garlic mixture, and stir. Add fresh herbs to heat through, then toss in cooked pasta, as well as the soy/rice parmesan and optional olive oil. Season with additional sea salt and black pepper if desired.
Makes 3-4 servings.

♥ For 4 servings, per serving (not including pasta): Calories: 147; Total Fat: 7.7 g (Sat. Fat: 0.9 g); Cholesterol: 0 mg; Carbohydrate: 13.7 g; Fiber: 1.8 g; Protein: 5.8 g.

Creamy Garlic Mushroom Sauce

3	whole bulbs roasted garlic (for tips on roasting garlic, see p. 33)
½ cup	vegetable stock
	dash of liquid smoke (optional)
1½-2 lbs	assorted mushrooms, sliced (e.g., portabella, oyster, shiitake, white button)
1½ tbsp	olive oil (for sauté)
1 cup	shallots or red onions, finely chopped
⅛-¼ tsp	sea salt
	fresh ground black pepper to taste
⅓ cup	white wine
1½-2 tbsp	fresh thyme or savory, chopped
3-4 tbsp	soy/rice parmesan
1 tbsp	olive oil (for finishing) (optional)

Squeeze garlic cloves from bulbs into vegetable stock. Add liquid smoke and, using a hand blender or in a food processor, purée the mixture and set aside. Discard any woody stems from mushrooms, and tear or slice mushrooms into pieces. In a large, deep skillet, heat the 1½ tbsp olive oil and sauté shallots or red onions over medium-high heat for 4-6 minutes, until they soften and are golden, seasoning with sea salt and pepper. Add mushrooms and cook for 6-7 minutes, tossing gently several times. Turn heat to high and add wine. Cook for a couple of minutes to allow some of the liquid to evaporate and alcohol to burn off. Once most of the liquid has evaporated, turn heat to medium-low, add puréed garlic mixture and fresh thyme or savory, and stir. Toss in soy/rice parmesan, optional olive oil, and cooked pasta just before serving. Season with additional sea salt and black pepper if desired.
Makes 3-4 servings.

♥ For 4 servings, per serving (not including pasta): Calories: 251; Total Fat: 10.2 g (Sat. Fat: 1.2 g); Cholesterol: 0 mg; Carbohydrate: 29.6 g; Fiber: 3.5 g; Protein: 9.8 g.

> *This is a delicious, exotic tasting sauce with an abundance of different mushrooms. If price or availability is a problem, you can use mushrooms such as white button.*

◆

> *Instead of pasta, serve this sauce over wild or basmati rice, along with a fresh salad, some crusty bread, or bruschetta.*

Creamy Garlic Tomato Sauce

3	whole bulbs roasted garlic (for tips on roasting garlic, see p. 33)
½ cup	vegetable stock
3 cups	tomatoes, seeded and chopped
1 tbsp	olive oil (for sauté)
⅛-¼ tsp	sea salt
	fresh ground black pepper to taste
⅓ cup	white wine
½ cup	green onions (green part only), chopped
1 tbsp	fresh thyme, chopped (see sidebar)
½ cup	fresh basil, chopped (see sidebar)
2-3 tbsp	soy/rice parmesan
1 tbsp	olive oil (for finishing) (optional)

Squeeze the garlic cloves from the bulbs into the vegetable stock. Using a hand blender or in a food processor, purée the mixture and set aside. In a saucepan, sauté tomatoes over medium-high heat in the 1 tbsp olive oil for 5-6 minutes, seasoning with sea salt and black pepper. Turn heat to high and add wine. Cook for a couple of minutes to allow some of the liquid to evaporate and the alcohol to burn off. Once most of the liquid has evaporated, turn heat to low, add puréed vegetable stock mixture, and stir. Stir in green onions and thyme, and after a minute stir in basil and soy/rice parmesan. Add cooked pasta immediately, so the fresh herbs do not fade with too much cooking. Season with additional sea salt and black pepper and toss in optional olive oil if desired. *Makes 3-4 servings.*

♥ For 4 servings, per serving (not including pasta): Calories: 160; Total Fat: 7.8 g (Sat. Fat: 1 g); Cholesterol: 0 mg; Carbohydrate: 16.9 g; Fiber: 2.4 g; Protein: 5.5 g.

Substitution note: You could use parsley or dill instead of basil, and fresh oregano in place of thyme.

For an added "kick," add a couple tbsp of pitted and chopped kalamata olives, and/or a couple tbsp of drained capers.

Mediterranean Sauce

1 tbsp	olive oil (to sauté)
½ cup	red onions, finely chopped
½ tsp	chili powder
¼ tsp	sea salt
	fresh ground black pepper to taste
1	28-oz can diced tomatoes, drained
5-7	garlic cloves, minced
½ cup	white wine
1 cup	artichoke hearts (from can or jar), drained, patted dry, and roughly chopped
¼ cup	kalamata and/or black olives, chopped
4-5 cups	fresh spinach, roughly chopped
1 cup	fresh basil leaves, packed, torn or cut into pieces
1 tbsp	olive oil (for finishing) (optional)
2-3 tbsp	fresh parsley, chopped, (for finishing) (optional)
1-2 tbsp	soy/rice parmesan (for finishing) (optional)

Colorful, flavorful, chunky, zesty: what more could you ask for in a pasta sauce?

In a saucepan, heat the 1 tbsp olive oil over medium heat. Add onions, chili powder, sea salt, and black pepper, and sauté for 4-5 minutes, until onions soften. Add tomatoes and garlic and cook for another 4-5 minutes. Turn heat to high and add wine. Cook for a minute or two, to allow some of the liquid to evaporate and the alcohol to burn off Reduce heat to low, add artichokes, olives, spinach, and basil. (Add spinach and basil just a few minutes before serving, so they won't overcook.) Toss for just a minute or two, until spinach wilts but is still bright green. Add cooked pasta immediately, as well as the optional 1 tbsp olive oil. Season with additional sea salt and black pepper and sprinkle with optional fresh parsley and soy/rice parmesan if desired.
Serves 4.

♥ For 4 servings, per serving (not including pasta): Calories: 218; Total Fat: 9 g (Sat. Fat: 1.1 g); Cholesterol: 0 mg; Carbohydrate: 26.2 g; Fiber: 8.4 g; Protein: 8.4 g.

Roasted Red Pepper Sauce

1 tbsp	olive oil (for sauté)
1 cup	shallots or red onions, roughly chopped
½ tsp	sea salt
	fresh ground black pepper, to taste
3-4	garlic cloves, roughly chopped
3	medium to large red peppers, roasted, skinned, and roughly chopped (for tips on roasting peppers, see p. 33)
¾-1 tsp	fresh rosemary, chopped
2 tsp	balsamic vinegar
½-¾ cup	fresh basil, chopped or torn into pieces
½ tbsp	olive oil (for finishing) (optional)

In a large saucepan, heat the 1 tbsp olive oil over medium heat. Add shallots, some of the salt, and a little black pepper, and sauté for 5-7 minutes, until shallots soften and start to brown. Add garlic and continue to sauté for another couple of minutes. Turn the heat to medium-low and add red peppers, rosemary, the remaining salt and another pinch of black pepper. Heat for 4-5 minutes, then using a hand blender or food processor, purée until smooth. Turn heat to low and stir in balsamic vinegar and basil. Add cooked pasta immediately, as well as the optional ½ tbsp olive oil. Season with additional sea salt and black pepper if desired. Do not mix in the basil until just before you are ready to serve, to retain its aroma and freshness.

Makes 3-4 servings.

♥ For 4 servings, per serving (not including pasta): Calories: 124; Total Fat: 5.3 g (Sat. Fat: 0.7 g); Cholesterol: 0 mg; Carbohydrate: 17.5 g; Fiber: 2.9 g; Protein: 1.5 g.

This sauce is smooth and creamy-rich-tasting. When red peppers are in season and not too pricey, this recipe is a must!

Black Bean Millet Patties

1½ tbsp	olive oil (for sauté)
1½ tbsp	ground cumin
2½ tsp	ground coriander
1½ tsp	ground fennel
2 tsp	mustard seeds
½ tsp	chili powder
	couple pinches red pepper flakes
½ cup	onions, finely chopped
2 tbsp	tahini
1-1½ tbsp	mild miso (e.g., brown rice miso)
3 cups	millet, cooked (see sidebar)
½ cup	black beans, cooked or canned
½ cup	celery, finely chopped
½ cup	sun-dried tomatoes, reconstituted and chopped
3-4 tbsp	raisins or currants
⅓-½ cup	fresh parsley, chopped
1 tsp	balsamic vinegar
¼ tsp	sea salt
	fresh ground black pepper to taste
¼-½ cup	coarse flour (e.g., Kamut), or other flour, for coating
	breadcrumbs or whole wheat flour (optional, see sidebar)
½ tbsp	olive oil (for frying)

You can substitute other cooked grains for the millet, such as quinoa, couscous, or brown rice. The ability of the patties to "bind" may depend on the grain when mixing the ingredients, so you may need to add extra tahini and/or some whole wheat flour or breadcrumbs to help the patties come together.

In a skillet, heat the 1½ tbsp olive oil over medium high heat. Add cumin, coriander, fennel, mustard seeds, chili powder, red pepper flakes, and a pinch of salt. Cook for a few minutes until very fragrant and the mustard seeds begin to pop. Add onions and stir. Reduce the heat a little and cook for another 3-4 minutes until onions soften a little. (You may want to add additional olive oil if the mixture is too dry.) Remove from heat and stir tahini and miso into the warm mixture. In a large mixing bowl, combine this mixture with remaining ingredients (except the coarse flour used to coat the patties) and mix well. If the mixture does not hold together when pressed, you may want to add a little whole wheat flour or breadcrumbs, or a little extra tahini. (Also, chilling the mixture a little before shaping the patties will help to keep them together.) Scoop mixture out with your hands to form patties (you may need to rinse your hands periodically to keep mixture from sticking to your hands). Once shaped, lightly coat patties in coarse flour. In a skillet coated with a little olive oil, fry patties over medium heat for 6-8 minutes on each side, until lightly browned *Makes 9-10 patties.*

♥ For 10 patties, per patty: Calories: 182; Total Fat: 5.6 g (Sat. Fat: 0.7 g); Cholesterol: 0 mg; Carbohydrate: 27.4 g; Fiber: 3.5 g; Protein: 5.4 g.

These patties are delicious on their own, but are also wonderful topped with a little sauce, such as "Tahini-Tamari Sauce" (p. 74), "Mi-so Good Gravy" (p. 72), some chutney, or even a plum or sweet and sour sauce.

Lentil Miso Patties

1 cup	dry, small red split lentils
1¾ cups	water
¼ tsp	ground fennel (optional)
1	whole bulb roasted garlic (for tips on roasting garlic, see p. 33)
1½-1¾ cups	good quality breadcrumbs
¾ cup	green onions, chopped
1 cup	red, yellow, or orange pepper, chopped
1 tbsp	hoisin sauce
2 tsp	seasoned rice vinegar
2½ tbsp	mild miso (e.g., brown rice miso)
1 tbsp	fresh ginger, minced
1 tbsp	olive oil
½ tsp	ground coriander
	fresh ground black pepper to taste
⅓ cup	flour (e.g., chickpea) (optional)

These patties are great served on their own (rather than as a "burger" with a bun), topped with "Mi-So Good Gravy" (p. 72) or "Sweet and Sour Sauce" (p. 138).

Rinse lentils well and add them to a large saucepan with water and optional ground fennel. Bring to a boil, then reduce heat to low and simmer partially covered for about 15 minutes, until liquid is absorbed and the lentils are soft. (For larger red lentils, similar to the size of green lentils, cook for 30-35 minutes.) Transfer cooked lentils to a mixing bowl. Squeeze roasted garlic from the bulb and mash into the lentils. Add remaining ingredients, and stir to combine well. If the mixture is not firm enough, add additional breadcrumbs or some flour. Place mixture in the refrigerator for about 1 hour, if possible, to help it to bind. Scoop mixture out with your hands to form into patties. For a crispier coating, use the optional flour to coat patties on each side before frying. In a skillet lightly coated with olive oil, fry patties on medium heat for 6-7 minutes on each side, until nicely browned.

Makes 9-10 patties.

♥ For 10 patties, per patty: Calories: 139; Total Fat: 2.7 g (Sat. Fat: 0.4 g); Cholesterol: 0 mg; Carbohydrate: 21.8 g; Fiber: 3.7 g; Protein: 7.3 g.

Roasted Red Pepper Dip (and) Roasted Eggplant Dip

SPICY THAI STEW

Cool Cucumber Tomato Toss

MUSHROOM PECAN BURGERS

GINGER HOISIN RICE NOODLES

Mediterranean Tortilla Pizzas

MEXICAN TOFU TACOS

BAKED LIME (OR LEMON!) "CREAM" PIE

"Lightened-Up" Falafels

Traditionally, falafels are deep-fried in oil, and while delicious, can be heavy to eat and high in fat. This version is lightened up with leafy herbs and crunchy celery, and pan-fried in just a smidgen of oil.

◆

Serve patties on their own, topped with "Tahini-Tamari Sauce" (p. 74), a nice twist from regular tahini sauce with the addition of tamari and a touch of toasted sesame oil. Another option is to serve them inside half a pita bread, with some lettuce, tomato, cucumber, any other fresh veggies you like, and drizzled with the tahini-tamari sauce.

2	14-oz cans chickpeas, rinsed and drained (roughly 3½ cups)
¼-⅓ cup	water
2 tbsp	lemon juice (preferably fresh)
1 tbsp	seasoned rice vinegar
3-4	garlic cloves, roughly chopped
1½ tsp	ground cumin
½ tsp	turmeric
½ tsp	ground coriander
½ tsp	sea salt
¾ cup	fresh parsley, packed
¼ cup	cilantro
¼-⅓ cup	red onions, finely chopped
½-¾ cup	celery, finely chopped
¼ cup	flour (e.g., chickpea)
⅓ cup	flour (e.g., chickpea) (for coating patties)

In a food processor, add chickpeas, water, lemon juice, rice vinegar, garlic, cumin, turmeric, coriander, and sea salt and purée until smooth, scraping down the sides of the food processor if needed. Add parsley and cilantro and continue to purée until mixture is chopped fairly well. Transfer mixture to a large mixing bowl, add onion and celery, and stir until well combined. Finally, stir in chickpea or other flour, again until well combined. Place mixture in the refrigerator for a half hour or more, if possible, to help it to bind. Scoop out mixture with your hands and form into patties. For a crispier coating, use the additional flour to coat patties on each side before frying. In a skillet lightly coated with olive oil, fry patties on medium heat for 6-8 minutes on each side, until lightly browned.

Makes 9-10 patties.

♥ For 10 patties, per patty: Calories: 128; Total Fat: 2 g (Sat. Fat: 0.2 g); Cholesterol: 0 mg; Carbohydrate: 20.9 g; Fiber: 5.3 g; Protein: 6.8 g.

Mushroom Pecan Burgers

1¼-1½ lbs	white mushrooms
½ cup	fresh parsley, packed
1-1½ cup	red or white onions, roughly chopped
2	medium-large garlic cloves, roughly chopped
1 tbsp	olive oil
3 tbsp	tahini
2 tbsp	hoisin sauce
¼ cup	toasted pecans or walnuts, chopped or lightly crushed (for tips on toasting nuts, see p. 36)
1 tbsp	balsamic vinegar
1 tsp	dried oregano
½ tsp	dried sage
¼ tsp	sea salt
	fresh ground black pepper to taste
2-2½ cups	good quality breadcrumbs

In a food processor, mince mushrooms with parsley (add mushrooms in 3 or 4 lots). Remove and set aside. In food processor, mince onion with garlic. If you don't have a food processor, chop these ingredients very finely by hand. In a saucepan over medium heat, sauté the garlic and onions with a pinch of sea salt and black pepper in olive oil for 5-6 minutes. In a large mixing bowl, mix all ingredients together (or first mix tahini and hoisin into the warm onion mixture, to help distribute it better). You will need to really work the mixture, applying pressure with your spoon until the texture holds together somewhat when pressed. Place mixture in the refrigerator for at least half an hour, if possible, to help it to bind. The mixture will be soft, but you will be able to form patties (if needed, add additional breadcrumbs and/or tahini). Scoop out mixture with your hands and form into patties. In a skillet lightly coated with oil, fry patties over medium heat for 5-7 minutes on each side until lightly browned and crispy on each side. Flip only once to keep patties intact.

Makes 10-12 patties.

♥ For 12 patties, per patty: Calories: 111; Total Fat: 5.5 g (Sat. Fat: 0.7 g); Cholesterol: 0 mg; Carbohydrate: 12.1 g; Fiber: 2.4 g; Protein: 3.4 g.

Simply delectable, moist, and savory patties - a sure favorite!

◆

Serve patties alone topped with "Mi-So Good Gravy" (p. 72), "Mushroom Gravy" (p. 73), along with a potato or rice dish and fresh salad. Or serve as you would a burger, in a roll or pita bread, with the usual fixings, such as tomato, lettuce, ketchup, and a dollop of Nayonnaise.

Next-Day Rice
(or Other Grain) Patties

2	whole bulbs roasted garlic (for tips on roasting garlic, see p. 33)
2 cups	grains, cooked (e.g., rice, millet, quinoa, etc.)
¾ cup	green onions, chopped
½ cup	bell pepper, finely chopped (any color)
¼ cup	celery, finely chopped
2 tbsp	tahini
1 tbsp	hoisin sauce
1 tbsp	rice vinegar
¼ tsp	chili powder
	few pinches sea salt
	fresh ground black pepper to taste
2-3 tbsp	fresh parsley, chopped (optional)
1-2 tbsp	whole wheat flour (optional)
¼-½ cup	coarse flour (e.g., Kamut)(optional)

In a large bowl, squeeze roasted garlic out of bulbs and mash a little. Add remaining ingredients (except for the whole wheat flour and optional coarse flour) and mix well. To firm up the mixture, add some whole wheat flour. Scoop out mixture with your hands and form into patties. For a crispier coating, use the coarse flour to coat patties on each side before frying. In a skillet lightly coated with oil, fry patties over medium heat for 6-7 minutes on each side, until lightly browned.

Makes 5-6 patties.

♥ For 6 patties, per patty: Calories: 188; Total Fat: 3.6 g (Sat. Fat: 0.5 g); Cholesterol: 0 mg; Carbohydrate: 33.2 g; Fiber: 4.1 g; Protein: 5.5 g.

These patties can be made quickly with leftover rice, especially a stickier one like brown rice. Other grains such as millet or quinoa can also be used for these delicious, easy veggie patties.

◆

Substitution note: Instead of roasted garlic, use 1-1½ tbsp of mild miso, and then for a hint of garlic, add one small to medium garlic clove, finely minced.

◆

Serve on its own, topped with "Sweet and Sour Sauce" (p. 138), "Mi-So Good Gravy" (p. 72), or your favorite condiments. Or serve in halved pita breads with your favorite "fixings".

Savory Tofu Burgers

1½ cups	red onions, finely chopped
½-1 tbsp	olive oil
	pinch of sea salt
	pinch of fresh ground black pepper
¼ cup	celery, finely chopped
1½ cups	mushrooms, finely chopped
1 tbsp	tamari (for sauté)
1	300-g pkg firm or extra-firm tofu, drained and squeezed dry (see tips on preparing tofu, see p. 31)
2	whole bulbs roasted garlic (for tips on roasting garlic, see p. 33)
1	156-ml can tomato paste (about ½ cup)
1-1¼ cups	good quality breadcrumbs
2-3 tbsp	dried savory
½-1 tbsp	tamari (to stir into mixture)
2 tsp	mild Dijon mustard
1 tsp	dried oregano
¾-1 tsp	chili powder

In a saucepan over medium heat, sauté onion in olive oil for 3-4 minutes, and season with salt and pepper. Add celery, mushrooms, and the 1 tbsp tamari, and continue to sauté for another 3-4 minutes until onions and celery soften. Remove from heat. Break tofu in chunks and in a food processor, purée until finely minced (alternatively, mash very finely). In a large mixing bowl, squeeze garlic from the bulb, and add sautéed mixture, minced tofu, and all other ingredients. Mix well. Mixture should be moist and hold together fairly well when pressure is applied. If it does not seem to be binding, add additional breadcrumbs and/or tomato paste. Scoop out mixture with your hands and form patties. In a skillet lightly coated with olive oil, fry patties over medium heat for 6-7 minutes on each side until lightly browned. *Makes 9-10 patties.*

♥ For 10 patties, per patty: Calories: 122; Total Fat: 4.6 g (Sat. Fat: 0.7 g); Cholesterol: 0 mg; Carbohydrate: 13.2 g; Fiber: 2.8 g; Protein: 6.9 g.

If you don't have time to roast garlic, try using a couple tbsp of a mild flavored miso, such as brown rice miso. It adds flavor as well as helps to bind the mixture. But since the miso is salty, omit the tamari.

◆

Serve these burgers on thinly sliced toasted rolls, in halved pita breads, or in flour tortillas, with your favorite burger fixings. They can also be served on own with salad and/or veggies, with "Mi-So Good Gravy" (p. 72).

Al's Creamy Mushroom Risotto

Risotto is a wonderful comfort food, rich in taste and texture, but usually made with butter, cream, and rich cheeses. This version is still creamy and delicious, thanks to the arborio rice itself and good olive oil. Combined with the mushrooms, peppers, and seasonings, this dish will become a decadent favorite!

◆

Substitution Idea: Experiment with the vegetables here, using mushrooms alone (5-6 cups) instead of red peppers, or combining varieties such as shiitake, button, and portabella. If you don't have fresh thyme, try substituting fresh oregano or a couple tbsp of fresh basil.

◆

Serve this risotto with "Best Bruschetta" (p. 60), a crunchy salad, and/or some lightly sautéed vegetables, such as asparagus or green beans, for a contrast in textures.

2 tbsp	olive oil (reserve ½ tbsp)
1 cup	red onions, chopped
	few pinches sea salt
	few pinches fresh ground black pepper
4 cups	mushrooms, thickly sliced (see sidebar)
3	large garlic cloves, minced
1 cup	arborio rice
3½-4 cups	vegetable stock
2	roasted red peppers, skins removed, and chopped (for tips on roasting red peppers, see p. 33)
¼ cup	green onions or chives, chopped
2 tsp	fresh thyme, chopped
1-1½ tbsp	soy/rice parmesan (optional)
	extra olive oil (for finishing) (optional)

In a large skillet, heat 1½ tbsp olive oil over medium heat. Add onions, a pinch of sea salt and black pepper, and sauté for 3-4 minutes. Add the mushrooms and garlic, another pinch of salt and pepper, and continue to sauté for another couple of minutes until the onions soften. Add rice, and reserved ½ tbsp olive oil, and stir well for 2-3 minutes. Add ½ cup vegetable stock and stir frequently until liquid is almost completely absorbed and the bottom of the pan starts to get dry. Then add another ½ cup stock, and again, stir until it is absorbed. Repeat this process (stirring almost continuously) until the rice reaches an "al dente" state (a slight firmness), roughly 20 minutes. You may not need the full 4 cups of stock, depending on the tenderness of the rice. Remove risotto from heat and stir in red pepper, green onions, thyme, and soy/rice parmesan. Finish with a drizzle of a little extra olive oil and stir. Season with additional sea salt and black pepper, and soy parmesan, if desired. Serve immediately.

Serves 3-4.

♥ For 4 servings, per serving: Calories: 331; Total Fat: 7.9 g (Sat. Fat: 1 g); Cholesterol: 0 mg; Carbohydrate: 55.6 g; Fiber: 4.9 g; Protein: 9.5 g.

"All Dressed" Squash

1	9-10 lb squash (buttercup, kabocha, sweet dumpling, or butternut) (or 2, 5-6 lb)
2 tbsp	olive oil (for sauté)
2 cups	onions, diced
½ tsp	sea salt (for sauté)
1 cup	celery, minced
5 cups	good quality breadcrumbs
½-¾ cup	apple, peeled and finely chopped
1 tsp	lemon juice, fresh squeezed
⅓-½ cup	dried cranberries
⅓ cup	dried savory
2-3 tsp	fresh thyme or oregano, chopped (optional)
¼ tsp	sea salt
	fresh ground black pepper to taste
¾ cup	vegetable stock
2 tbsp	olive oil

If using butternut squash, cut a lengthwise "top" off so it can sit on its side. There are fewer seeds and "strings" in butternut squash, so cut into the flesh to create a hollow large enough for stuffing.

For a great tasting, moist dressing, use regular good quality whole grain breads, even in combination with good quality white breads. The texture and taste of the stuffing depend a great deal on the bread itself. If you don't eat much white bread, you can enjoy a little here in this wonderful stuffing!

◆

This is fabulous served with "Mushroom Gravy" (p. 73) and cranberry sauce.

Preheat oven to 400°F. Place whole squash on upper rack of oven (place tinfoil or liner sheet on bottom rack to catch drippings) and bake for 40-50 minutes (less for two smaller squash), until a skewer or knife easily pierces the flesh. Remove from oven and let cool enough to handle. In the meantime, prepare other ingredients, leaving the apple last. In a skillet, heat the 2 tbsp olive oil over medium heat, and sauté onions and ½ tsp sea salt for 2-3 minutes, then add celery and continue to sauté for another 2-3 minutes, until the onions soften. In a large mixing bowl, combine onion/celery mixture with breadcrumbs. Toss apple in lemon juice and mix in, followed by cranberries, savory, optional thyme or oregano, remaining ¼ tsp sea salt, and black pepper to taste. Combine well, drizzle in stock and remaining 2 tbsp olive oil, and toss. The dressing should be fairly moist in spots, but not soggy or crumbly; if extra moisture is needed, add additional tbsp or two of olive oil and/or stock. Next, cut the top off of the squash (but don't discard) and scrape out seeds and stringy flesh, scraping into flesh a ½ inch or so (see sidebar). At this point, place squash in a baking dish that will encase it well, to stabilize it when you are moving it in and out of the oven. Scoop dressing into squash, patting it in lightly, and stuffing it very full. Replace top of squash and place back in oven and bake for another 35-45 minutes, until squash is very tender and the dressing is moist and fragrant.
Makes 6-8 servings.

♥ For 8 servings (including dressing), per serving: Calories: 437; Total Fat: 9.5 g (Sat. Fat: 1.5 g); Cholesterol: 0 mg; Carbohydrate: 75.6 g; Fiber: 13.3 g; Protein: 12 g.

Carrot Zucchini Crumb Casserole

1 cup	red onions, finely chopped
½ cup	celery, finely chopped
½ tbsp	olive oil
¾ cup	soft tofu
⅓ cup	Nayonnaise (or other creamy, not too tangy vegan mayonnaise)
2	large garlic cloves, roughly chopped
1 tsp	ground coriander
1-1½ tbsp	mild Dijon mustard
½ tsp	sea salt
⅛ tsp	fresh ground black pepper
3 cups	carrots, grated (food processor is easiest)
2 cups	zucchini, grated (food processor is easiest)

TOPPING:

2 cups	good quality breadcrumbs, packed
¼ cup	sesame seeds
1 tsp	mild Dijon mustard
½ tbsp	olive oil

Preheat oven to 375°F. In a saucepan, sauté onion and celery in the ½ tbsp olive oil over medium heat for 5-6 minutes until just softened, and season with pinch of sea salt and black pepper. Remove from heat and set aside. In food processor, purée tofu and add Nayonnaise, garlic, coriander, mustard, sea salt, and pepper, scraping down the sides of the food processor. In a large bowl, combine carrots and zucchini with tofu mixture, onions and celery, and mix well. Transfer to a lightly oiled 8"x12" baking dish. Combine ingredients for the topping and mix together with your hands. Sprinkle topping evenly over vegetable mixture and press it down lightly. Bake for 28-30 minutes, until the casserole bubbles around the edges and the topping is golden brown.
Serves 5.

♥ For 5 servings, per serving: Calories: 239; Total Fat: 12 g (Sat. Fat: 1.8 g); Cholesterol: 0 mg; Carbohydrate: 25.5 g; Fiber: 5.9 g; Protein: 7.6 g.

ornmeal Chili Bake

Cornmeal Topping:

3 cups	water
1 tsp	sea salt
1 cup	quick-cooking cornmeal
1 tbsp	olive oil
½ tsp	oregano
⅛ tsp	cumin
⅛ tsp	chili powder
	couple pinches turmeric
1 tbsp	soy/rice parmesan (optional)

Chili: (see sidebar)

1½-2 tsp	olive oil
1 cup	onions, chopped
⅛ tsp	sea salt
½-¾ cup	celery, chopped
½ cup	carrots, chopped
2	medium-large garlic cloves, minced
1 tsp	chili powder
¼ tsp	dried oregano
¼ tsp	cumin
¾ cup	bell peppers, chopped (any color)
½ cup	corn kernels or zucchini
1	14-oz can beans of choice, drained and rinsed (roughly 1-1½ cups) (see sidebar)
1	28-oz can diced tomatoes (do not drain)
¼ cup	tomato paste (preferably spicy or garlic)
1 tsp	dark soy sauce or tamari
	dash of hot sauce (optional)
¼ tsp	unrefined, white or brown sugar
¼ cup	cilantro or parsley, chopped (optional)
	extra sea salt to taste
	extra fresh ground black pepper to taste

For the chili, you can either make this recipe or simply use 4½ to 5 cups of canned or frozen veggie chili. Follow the directions for the cornmeal topping, and you will transform regular chili into a new meal!

◆

Instead of beans, you could use marinated, minced tofu, or texturized vegetable protein (TVP).

FOR THE TOPPING:

In a medium pot, bring water and sea salt to a boil. Lower heat and slowly whisk in cornmeal until thickened, about 2-3 minutes. Add remaining ingredients and stir well. Season with additional sea salt and black pepper if desired. Cover and cool a little.

FOR THE CHILI:

In a saucepan, heat olive oil over medium heat and add onions and sea salt. Cover and cook for 2-3 minutes, stirring occasionally. Add celery and carrots, cover and cook for another 2-3 minutes, stirring occasionally. Add garlic, chili powder, oregano, and cumin, stir and cook for another 2-3 minutes. Add peppers, corn, beans, diced tomatoes, tomato paste, soy sauce, optional hot sauce, and sugar. Bring up to a boil, then reduce heat to medium-low, cover, and let simmer covered for 13-15 minutes. Remove lid and let reduce for 3-5 minutes, until the chili has thickened a little. Remove from heat and stir in optional cilantro or parsley. Season with additional sea salt and black pepper if desired.

Preheat oven to 375°F. Spoon chili into an 8" x 12" baking dish. Spoon cornmeal mixture over the chili entirely, or preferably, pipe the mixture on: either use a pastry bag, or spoon mixture into a clean plastic bag and cut a small ¼" hole in the corner; tighten bag around mixture to pipe it through the hole. Sprinkle with additional soy/rice parmesan if desired, and bake for 28-30minutes, until cornmeal has started to brown and chili is bubbling.
Makes 5-6 servings.

♥ For 6 servings, per serving: Calories: 273; Total Fat: 5.5 g (Sat. Fat: 0.8 g); Cholesterol: 0 mg; Carbohydrate: 46.2 g; Fiber: 10.1 g; Protein: 9.9 g.

For the topping, consider substituting cornmeal with mashed potatoes or yams, particularly if you have leftovers you want to use. You can still season them with the same ingredients, omitting the turmeric.

Creamy Potato Leek Bake

4 cups	all-purpose or Russet potatoes, skinned and cubed
	cold water (enough to cover potatoes)
	couple pinches sea salt
1 tbsp	olive oil (for sauté)
4½-5 cups	leeks, chopped (white portion, and some of the light green)
1-2 tbsp	olive oil (to mix into mashed potatoes)
4-5 tbsp	plain soy milk
2 tbsp	soy/rice parmesan (optional)
¼ tsp	sea salt
2	whole bulbs roasted garlic (for tips on roasting garlic, see p. 33)
	fresh ground black pepper to taste
	extra soy/rice parmesan for sprinkling (optional)

FOR SAUCE:

1 cup	vegetable stock, cold or room temperature
1½ tbsp	arrowroot flour
1 tbsp	tamari or soy sauce
½ tsp	molasses
¼ tsp	dried thyme
¼ tsp	dried oregano
¼ tsp	dried savory

> This is a great recipe to use leftover mushroom gravy. Instead of the sauce mixture, use 1-1¼ cups mushroom gravy to mix with the leeks.

Place potatoes in a pot, cover with cold water, and add a couple of pinches sea salt. Bring to a boil, then reduce heat to low and let simmer, covered, for 18-20 minutes, or until tender. While potatoes are cooking, in a large skillet, heat the 1 tbsp olive oil over medium heat. Add leeks and a pinch of sea salt and black pepper and sauté for 8-10 minutes, until leeks are soft and wilted (if the leeks stick to the pan, add a little water and reduce heat). While leeks are cooking, prepare the sauce mixture. In a small bowl, combine a few tbsps vegetable stock with arrowroot flour, stirring until very smooth. Then work mixture back into remaining vegetable stock, stirring to combine well. Add remaining sauce ingredients into vegetable stock and stir through. When leeks are cooked, add sauce mixture into the skillet. Turn the heat up to high to bring just to a boil, then remove from heat. When potatoes are cooked, drain and mash them with remaining ½ tbsp olive oil, soy milk or water (if your potatoes are somewhat dry, use the full 3 tbsps, or even a little more), optional soy/rice parmesan, the ¼ tsp sea salt, and black pepper. When almost smooth, lightly mash in the roasted garlic cloves (they should still be a bit chunky in the potatoes). Spoon potato mixture into a lightly oiled 8"x12" baking dish and spread out evenly. Pour leek and sauce mixture over potato mixture and spread out evenly. (see sidebar) Sprinkle top with extra soy parmesan if desired, then bake for 21-22 minutes at 375°F until golden brown in spots and a little bubbly in the corners.

Makes 4-5 servings.

♥ For 5 servings, per serving: Calories: 274; Total Fat: 9.1 g (Sat. Fat: 1.1 g); Cholesterol: 0 mg; Carbohydrate: 42.1 g; Fiber: 4.1 g; Protein: 5.9 g.

For a delicious crunchy topping, toss 1-1¼ cups of breadcrumbs with 2-3 tsps of olive oil, and sprinkle over top before baking.

Ginger Hoisin Rice Noodles

SAUCE:

¼ cup	hoisin sauce
2 tsp	tamari
3 tbsp	fresh ginger, minced
2-3	medium-large garlic cloves, minced
¼ cup	seasoned rice vinegar
2-3 tbsp	toasted sesame oil
1 tsp	ground coriander
⅛-¼ tsp	red pepper flakes

NOODLES AND VEGGIES:

½ lb	dry rice vermicelli or other thin rice noodles (about ½ of a 16-oz. package)
	cold water (enough to boil noodles)
½ tbsp	olive oil
1	large carrot, julienned
1-2	large celery stalks, thinly sliced on diagonal
1	medium red pepper, thinly sliced
1	small yellow or green pepper, thinly sliced
1-1½ cups	green onions, thinly sliced on diagonal
¼-⅓ cup	fresh parsley, finely chopped
⅓-½ cup	cilantro, finely chopped
1-3 tbsp	water (optional)
	sea salt to taste
	fresh ground black pepper to taste
	several lemon wedges (for finishing)
	extra toasted sesame oil (for finishing) (optional)

In a bowl, combine all ingredients for the sauce, stir well, and set aside. Prepare a pot of boiling water, and add noodles when ready (follow package directions). While waiting for the water to boil, in a skillet over medium heat, heat olive oil. Add carrots, celery, and any whitish portions of the green onions, a couple pinches sea salt, and let cook for a couple of minutes. Add noodles to boiling water, if ready. In the skillet, add peppers and toss for a minute or two. Reduce heat to medium-low and add sauce mixture, along with remaining green onions, parsley, and cilantro. Remove from heat if waiting for noodles. Once noodles are cooked, drain and add them to vegetable mixture. Toss to evenly distribute vegetables and sauce throughout noodles. If mixture is a little dry, add the 1-3 tbsp water, and/or extra sesame oil. Finish to taste with sea salt, black pepper, a squeeze of lemon juice, and an extra drizzle of sesame oil. *Makes 4 servings.*

♥ For 4 servings, per serving: Calories: 408; Total Fat: 13 g (Sat. Fat: 1.9 g); Cholesterol: 0 mg; Carbohydrate: 67.4 g; Fiber: 5 g; Protein: 5 g.

"Grate" Potato Bake

2½ lbs	Russet potatoes, peeled and thickly grated
1¼-1½ cups	red onions, thinly sliced
1 tsp	dry mustard
2 tsp	dried dill
¾ tsp	sea salt
	fresh ground black pepper to taste
1½ cups	plain soy milk
1-1¼ cups	breadcrumbs
2-3 tsp	olive oil

Preheat oven to 400°F. In a large bowl, combine all ingredients except soy milk, breadcrumbs and olive oil, and toss well. Transfer mixture to a lightly oiled 8"x12" baking dish. Pour soy milk over the top, and lightly press down mixture with the back of a large spoon or spatula. Combine breadcrumbs with olive oil, and sprinkle them over the top. Cover with tin foil and bake for 35-40 minutes, then remove foil and continue to bake for 20-25 minutes, until potatoes are tender and topping is nicely browned.
Makes 4-5 servings.

♥ For 5 servings, per serving: Calories: 288; Total Fat: 5 g (Sat. Fat: 0.8 g); Cholesterol: 0 mg; Carbohydrate: 51.9 g; Fiber: 6.4 g; Protein: 8.7 g.

This dish is excellent with a sauce such as "Creamy Dijon Dill Dressing" (p. 77), "Tahini-Tamari Sauce" (p. 74), "Mi-So Good Gravy" (p. 72), or "Avocado Roasted Garlic Sauce" (p. 71). Serve along with a generous, crunchy salad and/or lightly sautéed or steamed veggies.

Mediterranean Tortilla Pizzas

4	large tortilla shells
1¼ cups	pasta sauce
1	156-ml can tomato paste (roughly ½ cup)
1 cup	fresh basil, roughly chopped or torn
3	whole bulbs roasted garlic (for tips on roasting garlic, see p. 33)
⅓ cup	shallots or red onions, finely minced
¾ cup	sun-dried tomatoes, reconstituted and chopped
2	170-ml jars marinated artichokes (about 1¼ cups), drained, patted dry, and sliced in half
3	roasted red peppers, skins removed and sliced (for tips on roasting peppers, see p. 33) (see sidebar)
2-2½ tbsp	rice/soy parmesan (optional)
	fresh ground black pepper to taste
	fresh parsley or basil (garnish) (optional)
	olive oil (for finishing) (optional)

These pizzas are perfect for thin-crust lovers (like me!). The tortilla shells get nice and crispy, and the toppings are chunky and zesty.

◆

If you don't have time to roast peppers, slice them fresh and soak for 10-15 minutes in 1 tbsp balsamic vinegar and a pinch of sea salt and black pepper. They will absorb some of the vinegar which imparts a nice flavor to the pizzas.

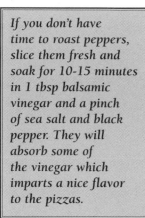

Preheat oven to 375°F. On two baking sheets, place tortilla shells and bake for 8-10 minutes (rotate sheets halfway through) until lightly golden and crispy. Watch shells closely, they can burn quickly. Remove from oven to cool. Mix pasta sauce with tomato paste and basil, and spread over cooled tortillas. Squeeze roasted garlic from bulbs. Spread garlic, shallots, sun-dried tomatoes, artichokes, and red peppers over each shell, and sprinkle with optional rice/soy parmesan. Season with black pepper to taste. Return to oven and bake at 375°F for 12-15 minutes (again rotating the trays halfway through), until toppings start to lightly brown. Remove from oven and sprinkle with optional fresh herbs and olive oil if desired.

Makes 4 pizzas.

♥ For 4 pizzas, per pizza: Calories: 462; Total Fat: 9.5 g (Sat. Fat: 1.1 g); Cholesterol: 0 mg; Carbohydrate: 78.6 g; Fiber: 10.8 g; Protein: 15.3 g.

Mexican Tofu Tacos

1 tbsp	dark soy sauce or tamari
1 tbsp	balsamic vinegar
½-1 tsp	chipotle hot sauce (or other hot sauce, adjust to taste)
1½ cups	firm or extra-firm tofu, mashed until somewhat crumbly (see tips on preparing tofu, p. 31)
½ tbsp	olive oil
½ cup	carrots, finely chopped
½ cup	celery, finely chopped
1½ tsp	chili powder
1 tsp	ground cumin
	couple pinches sea salt
	couple pinches fresh ground black pepper
1¼-1½ cups	green or red pepper, finely chopped
½ cup	fresh or frozen corn kernels (optional)
1 cup	tomatoes, seeded and chopped
½ cup	pasta sauce
½ cup	salsa
1 tbsp	tomato paste
¼ cup	green onions, chopped
¼ cup	fresh cilantro or parsley, chopped (optional)
10 (or more) taco shells	

OPTIONAL GARNISHES:

avocado, chopped or mashed (or guacamole)

jicama, chopped

soy cheese, grated

lettuce, shredded

"Hot Nacho Dip" (p. 62)

"Creamy Dijon Dill Dressing" (p. 77)

> Substitution note: Instead of taco shells, you could use warmed flour tortillas, pita breads, or even top rice or potatoes with this mixture. The taco shells are best when warmed in the oven for a few minutes.

In a bowl, mix soy sauce, balsamic vinegar, and hot sauce, then add tofu and mix through. In a large skillet, heat olive oil over medium heat. Add tofu, carrots, celery, chili powder, cumin, and a pinch of sea salt and black pepper, and cook for 5-7 minutes, stirring several times. Add peppers, corn, tomatoes, pasta sauce, salsa, and tomato paste, and cook for 4-5 minutes, stirring several times. If there is still moisture, cook for another couple of minutes until liquid evaporates. Stir in green onions and optional cilantro/parsley a few minutes before serving to heat through. If not serving right away, reserve green onions and herbs to add before serving. Season with additional sea salt and black pepper if desired. Spoon mixture into taco shells, and top with optional garnishes. *Makes 10 or more tacos.*

♥ For 10 tacos (optional garnishes not included), per taco: Calories: 148; Total Fat: 6.8 g (Sat. Fat: 0.8 g); Cholesterol: 0 mg; Carbohydrate: 16.6 g; Fiber: 2.4 g; Protein: 5.3 g.

The taco filling can be easily stored in the refrigerator to reheat for another night. It's a great quick meal for a group.

Phyllo Spinach Pie ("Spanokopita")

1½ tbsp	olive oil (for sauté)
1¾ cups	red onion, finely chopped
4-5	garlic cloves, minced
¼ tsp	sea salt
	fresh ground pepper to taste
1	300-g pkg frozen spinach, thawed, or 8-9 cups fresh spinach, packed, roughly chopped
¾ cup	extra-firm or firm tofu, finely minced (food processor is easiest) (see tips on preparing tofu, p. 31)
¼ cup	fresh dill, finely chopped
3 tbsp	soy/rice parmesan
2 tsp	lemon juice (preferably freshly squeezed)
4-5 tsp	rice vinegar (preferably seasoned)
11-12	full sheets phyllo pastry
3 tbsp	olive oil (or oil spritzer) (to brush pastry)

This is a wonderful alternative to the traditional spanokopita, which is heavy with feta cheese and sometimes eggs. The tofu is minced until it is almost powder fine, so it is not tasteless and chunky as some vegan versions of this recipe can be. This does take a little longer to make than other recipes here, but it's well worth it!

Preheat oven to 350°F. In a skillet, heat the 1½ tbsp olive oil over medium heat. Add onions, garlic, sea salt, and black pepper and sauté for 6-7 minutes, until onions are soft and translucent. Remove from heat and let cool while preparing the other ingredients. If using frozen spinach which has been thawed, place it in a colander and squeeze out as much liquid as possible. (If using fresh spinach, place it in a colander with a bowl underneath and pour boiling water over to blanch it. Repeat process until spinich is just wilted, which should take a minute or two. Rinse spinach under cold water, then squeeze well to remove as much liquid as possible.) Roughly chop spinach. In a large mixing bowl, combine all ingredients (except the phyllo pastry and the 3 tbsp olive oil), and mix very well. Let mixture cool a little before layering pastry.

Lightly oil an 8"x12" baking dish. To layer the phyllo, take the full sheets of pastry and cut them in half along the longest side so that once cut, the half sheets will fit your baking dish. (If using another size dish, cut your phyllo sheets accordingly to fit your dish, keeping in mind that you may need more than 12 sheets.) Brush or spray a half sheet with a little of the 3 tbsp olive oil, then layer with another sheet and repeat process. Continue until you have 5 sheets layered (you do not need to brush the 5th sheet, since it will have the filling placed on it). Place layered sheets on bottom of baking dish. Distribute about ⅓ of your filling over the layer of pastry. Prepare another layer of phyllo sheets, this time using 4 sheets, then layer with another ⅓ of filling. Repeat with another layer of 4 sheets, and finally the last ⅓ of filling. Place one sheet of phyllo and place this on top of the last layer of filling. To top the dish, brush each last sheet of phyllo with olive oil. Gently bring the edges of each sheet together with your fingertips to make loose wrinkles. Place each wrinkled sheet on top of dish, filling the entire surface area. You should be able to fit 8-9 half sheets on top like this. Don't worry about it being perfect, the idea is to have a decorative look, and the wrinkled sheets will look beautiful when baked. Trim around edge of pie with a sharp knife to remove any extra phyllo. Bake for 23-25 minutes, until the pastry is nicely browned. (If refrigerating before baking, cover with plastic wrap; once chilled, your baking time will be a bit longer.)
Makes 5 servings.

♥ For 5 servings, per serving: Calories: 380; Total Fat: 16.3 g (Sat. Fat: 2.2 g); Cholesterol: 0 mg; Carbohydrate: 46.2 g; Fiber: 4.2 g; Protein: 12.2 g.

This pie is nice served with a fresh, crunchy salad topped with "Creamy Dijon Dill Dressing" (p. 77) or "Lemon Curry Dressing" (p. 78). And extra dressing to drizzle over the pie to moisten it is quite delicious!

Roasted Veggie Feast

2	medium-large red or yellow peppers, cut in chunks
1	medium-large green pepper, cut in chunks
6	medium-large tomatoes (preferably Roma), seeded and cut in chunks
1	large red onion, cut in chunks
1 lb	mushrooms (e.g., button, portabella), thickly sliced
1	fennel bulb, cut in chunks
8-10	garlic cloves, cut in chunks
3 tbsp	olive oil
1 tbsp	dark soy sauce or tamari
2-2½ tbsp	fresh thyme, chopped (or 2-2½ tsp dried) (see sidebar)
¼ tsp	sea salt
¼ tsp	fresh ground black pepper
2	Japanese eggplant, halved and cut in 1" pieces (see sidebar)
1 tbsp	balsamic vinegar (for finishing)
¼ cup	fresh parsley, basil, or coriander, chopped (garnish) (optional)

Japanese eggplant (sometimes called Chinese eggplant) is a long, light purple variety, similar in shape to zucchini. Its flavor is often preferred to that of the larger, bulbous dark purple eggplants, which can be bitter. If you are unable to find Japanese eggplant, use 1 medium-large (roughly 1 lb) regular eggplant and cut into 1" cubes.

Substitution ideas: Instead of the thyme, try fresh oregano or rosemary (use only 1-1½ tbsp of rosemary). Zucchini can be used in lieu of eggplant. You could also try asparagus and/or green beans; these are delicious when roasted, however, they need less cooking time, so add them in the last 15-20 minutes of cooking. Potatoes and yams could also be used, but these need to be cubed in pieces no larger than 1", in order to cook in the same time as the other veggies.

Preheat oven to 425°F. In a large bowl, combine all vegetables except eggplant. Add olive oil, soy sauce, thyme, sea salt, and black pepper, and mix well. Add eggplant and continue to mix. If veggies appear to need extra oil, add a couple dashes. Line two baking sheets with parchment paper (or lightly oil them). Spoon out veggies evenly between the two trays. Bake for 35-40 minutes, rotating the trays halfway through baking. Remove from oven. Transfer veggies to a large serving bowl. Sprinkle on balsamic vinegar, optional fresh herbs, and toss. Season further with sea salt and black pepper if desired.

Makes 4-5 servings as an entrée with a grain or pasta.

♥ For 5 servings (vegetables only), per serving: Calories: 258; Total Fat: 9.6 g (Sat. Fat: 1.3 g); Cholesterol: 0 mg; Carbohydrate: 36 g; Fiber: 11 g; Protein: 7.2 g.

Serve the vegetables on their own, or on top of grains, potatoes, or pasta. Leftovers can be used to make a very quick pizza: use your favorite crust and tomato sauce topping, and add the veggies. Sprinkle on a little soy/rice parmesan, and bake for 8-10 minutes at 375°F.

Spiced Mushroom Potato Phyllo Pie

2 tbsp	olive oil (for sauté)
1½ cups	red onions, chopped
¼-½ tsp	sea salt
2 tsp	fenugreek
1½ tsp	ground coriander
1 tsp	mustard seeds
½ tsp	turmeric
½ tsp	ground fennel
	fresh ground black pepper to taste
1½-1¾ cups	(about ¾ lb) all-purpose potatoes, cubed
1-2 tbsp	water
6 cups	(about 1-1¼ lb) white button mushrooms, sliced
1½-2 tbsp	fresh ginger, grated
1-1½ tsp	lemongrass, finely chopped (see sidebar)
1 tbsp	arrowroot flour, dissolved in 1-2 tbsp water
1-2 tsp	hoisin sauce
¼ cup	fresh parsley, finely chopped (optional)
14-16	sheets phyllo pastry
3 tbsp	olive oil (or oil spritzer) (to brush phyllo)

Instead of lemongrass, you could use lemon zest or fresh lemon juice.

In a large pot, heat the 2 tbsp olive oil over medium heat. Add onions, salt, fenugreek, ground coriander, mustard seeds, turmeric, ground fennel, and black pepper, and cook for a few minutes. Add potatoes and water, reduce heat to medium-low, cover and let simmer for 6-7 minutes. Stir in mushrooms, increase heat a little, cover and cook for 6-7 minutes. Stir in ginger and lemongrass, cover again and cook for a few minutes. Check potatoes; if they are not tender, continue cooking for another few minutes. When potatoes are tender, stir in arrowroot/water mixture until mixture thickens. Stir in hoisin sauce and parsley, and remove the pot from the heat. Allow mixture to cool before layering the phyllo.

To assemble the pie:

Preheat oven to 350°F. Lightly oil an 8"x12" baking dish. To layer the phyllo, take the full sheets of pastry and cut them in half along the longest side so that once cut, the half sheets will fit your baking dish. (If using another size dish, cut your phyllo sheets accordingly to fit your dish, keeping in mind that you may need more than 12 sheets.) Brush or spray a half sheet with a little of the 3 tbsp olive oil, then layer with another sheet and repeat process. Continue until you have 5 sheets layered (you do not need to brush the 5th sheet, since it will have the filling placed on it). Place layered sheets on bottom of baking dish. Distribute about ⅓ of cooled mushroom-potato filling over the layer of pastry. Prepare another layer of phyllo sheets, this time using 4 sheets, then layer with another ⅓ of filling. Repeat with another layer of 4 sheets, and finally the last ⅓ of filling. Place one sheet of phyllo and place this on top of the last layer of filling. To top the dish, brush each last sheet of phyllo with olive oil. Gently bring the edges of each sheet together with your fingertips to make loose wrinkles. Place each wrinkled sheet on top of dish, filling the entire surface area. You should be able to fit 8-9 half sheets on top like this. Don't worry about it being perfect, the idea is to have a decorative look, and the wrinkled sheets will look beautiful when baked. Trim around edge of pie with a sharp knife to remove any excess phyllo, and sprinkle top with a little ground coriander if desired. Bake for 23-27 minutes, until the pastry is golden brown. (If refrigerating before baking, cover with plastic wrap; once chilled, your baking time will be a bit longer.)
Makes 5-6 servings.

♥ For 6 servings, per serving: Calories: 403; Total Fat: 13.6 g (Sat. Fat: 1.8 g); Cholesterol: 0 mg; Carbohydrate: 60.9 g; Fiber: 4.6 g; Protein: 9.1 g.

Sweet and Sour "Neat" Balls

SWEET AND SOUR SAUCE: (SEE SIDEBAR)

2½ tbsp	arrowroot flour
1½ cups	water
½ cup	unrefined or brown sugar
½ cup	ketchup
½ cup	rice vinegar
2 tbsp	tamari or soy sauce
1 tsp	fresh ginger, grated (or ¼ tsp dried ginger)
	couple dashes cayenne

TOFU BALLS:

2 cups	(300 g pkg) extra-firm or firm tofu, finely minced (food processor is easiest) (see tips on preparing tofu, p. 31)
1 cup	good quality breadcrumbs
½ cup	red onions, minced
½ cup	celery, minced
¼ cup	carrots, minced
¼ cup	fresh coriander or parsley, finely chopped
3 tbsp	hoisin sauce
2½ tbsp	brown rice miso (or another mild miso)
2 tbsp	whole wheat flour
2 tsp	toasted sesame oil
⅛ tsp	fresh ground black pepper
1	whole bulb roasted garlic (for tips on roasting garlic, see p. 33)

Time saver tip: You can use a bottled sweet and sour sauce as an option to preparing this one. Also, rather than making the tofu balls, you could use strips of fried tofu. But I must admit that these "neat" balls always get rave reviews, so they are well worth the preparation!

FOR THE SAUCE:

Completely dissolve arrowroot in water, stirring well until very smooth. In a saucepan, combine this with the other ingredients. Bring mixture to a boil, stirring frequently, particularly once the sauce begins to thicken. Once it reaches a boil, remove from heat and serve, or cover with a lid until ready to serve. Season with sea salt and black pepper if desired.

FOR THE TOFU BALLS:

Preheat oven to 400°F. In a large bowl, combine all ingredients and mix well, pressing mixture slightly. The mixture should hold together fairly well when pressed down. If it is still a little moist, add another teaspoon or two of whole wheat flour, and if it needs to bind more, add a little extra miso or hoisin (not too much or they will be salty). The more you work with and press the mixture, the better it will bind to form the balls. Scoop mixture with your hands and form into golf ball-sized balls (will yield roughly 19-20 balls). Place on a baking sheet lightly oiled or lined with parchment paper. If you have an olive oil spritzer, spritz the tofu balls lightly with oil before baking. Bake for 19-22 minutes until lightly browned.

When serving, do not mix the tofu balls into the sweet and sour sauce, as they can easily crumble. Rather, serve them over rice, veggies, or on their own (see sidebar), then coat generously with the sauce.

Makes 4-5 servings.

♥ For 4 tofu balls (with ½ cup of sauce), per serving: Calories: 331; Total Fat: 8.9 g (Sat. Fat: 1.6 g); Cholesterol: 0 mg; Carbohydrate: 49.3 g; Fiber: 3.6 g; Protein: 13.1 g.

This is wonderful served over "Baked Herbed Spaghetti Squash" (p. 146), as the tofu balls are quite substantial and the squash is a light complement. Other accompaniments might be the "Roasted Turnip Purée" (p. 155) or "Yam Purée" (p. 159). Or try serving them over couscous, quinoa, or wild or brown rice, with a mixed green salad or lightly sautéed fresh vegetables.

Tarragon Jewel Acorn Squash

4	*acorn squash (about 1½ lbs. each)*
2½ cups	*cooked rice, cool or warm*
1½ cups	*tomatoes, seeded and chopped*
½ cup	*fresh or frozen corn*
½ cup	*green onions, chopped*
¼ cup	*celery, chopped*
3 tbsp	*toasted pine nuts (for tips on toasting nuts, see p. 36)*
2 tbsp	*currants*
2-2½ tsp	*fresh tarragon, chopped*
1	*small-medium garlic cloves, minced*
2 tsp	*lemon juice (preferably freshly squeezed)*
½-1 tsp	*lemon zest*
⅛ tsp	*fresh ground black pepper*
	couple pinches cinnamon
½ tsp	*sea salt*
2 tsp	*maple syrup (for filling)*
2-3 tsp	*maple syrup (for squash)*
	several lemon wedges (garnish) (optional)

Preheat oven to 400°F. Place squash whole on top oven rack, with aluminum foil below to catch drippings. Bake for 40-45 minutes, until squash are soft when pierced. Remove from oven to cool while preparing stuffing. In a large bowl, combine all ingredients except salt and the 2-3 tsp maple syrup. (Mix in salt just before stuffing squash.) Remove stems from the bottom of squash so that they will stand easily. Slice the opposite end (pointy tops) from squash (about 1-2"), reserving the tops. Scoop out seeds and scrape cavity clean. Arrange squash in a baking dish. Use the reserved 2-3 tsp maple syrup and rub it in the cavity of each squash, and flesh side of squash tops. Spoon mixture into each squash evenly, press in lightly, and drizzle a little extra maple syrup over top. Replace squash tops to cover. Cover baking dish with aluminum foil and bake for 35-40 minutes, then remove foil and squash tops and bake for an additional 5 minutes to lightly brown the filling. Replace the squash tops to serve, along with a lemon wedge and extra sea salt and black pepper, to season.

One squash can be served per person; however, they are fairly substantial, so depending on your menu, they could make 4-6 servings or more.

♥ For 4 squashes, per squash: Calories: 593; Total Fat: 5.4 g (Sat. Fat: 0.9 g); Cholesterol: 0 mg; Carbohydrate: 123.7 g; Fiber: 15.6 g; Protein: 12 g.

Thick 'n' Juicy Pesto Portabellas

2-3	*large portabella mushrooms (about 1¼ lbs total)*
½ tsp	*olive oil*
	couple pinches sea salt
	couple pinches fresh ground black pepper
1 cup	*spinach, packed*
1	*(170-ml) jar marinated artichokes, drained and patted dry*
½ cup	*"Best-o Pesto Sauce" (p. 104)*
2 tbsp	*Nayonnaise (or other creamy, not too tangy vegan mayonnaise)*
¼ cup	*good quality breadcrumbs*
½ cup	*good quality breadcrumbs*
½ tbsp	*soy/rice rice parmesan (for finishing)*

Preheat oven to 400°F. With a damp cloth or paper towel, clean mushroom caps. Remove stems and with the tip of a large spoon, scrape gills out from the underside. Rub outside of caps with olive oil, season with sea salt and black pepper, and place with oiled side down on a baking sheet. To make filling, roughly chop spinach and artichokes, and combine in a bowl with pesto, Nayonnaise, and the ¼ cup of breadcrumbs. Fill caps with the mixture to heaping. Combine remaining ½ cup breadcrumbs with soy parmesan and sprinkle evenly over filling. Season with black pepper. Bake for 12-14 minutes, until topping starts to brown. *Serves 2-3 as an entrée. (see sidebar)*

♥ For 3 servings, per serving: Calories: 312; Total Fat: 11.2 g (Sat. Fat: 1.4 g); Cholesterol: 0 mg; Carbohydrate: 39.3 g; Fiber: 5.9 g; Protein: 13.4 g.

These delicious stuffed mushrooms can be served as an entrée or side dish, or can be cut into smaller pieces for a wonderful appetizer for 6-8 people.

Tomato-Olive Rice Bake

½ cup	tomato paste
3	medium-large garlic cloves, minced
1 tsp	molasses
1½ tsp	dried oregano
½-¾ tsp	sea salt
⅛ tsp	fresh ground black pepper
3 cups	cooked brown/wild rice mixture (see sidebar)
2 cups	fresh spinach, packed and roughly chopped
1 cup	bell peppers, chopped (any color)
1	28-oz can diced tomatoes, drained
½ cup	red onions, finely chopped
⅓ cup + 1 tbsp fresh dill, finely chopped (or 1 tbsp dried)	
¼ cup	kalamata and/or black olives, chopped
1 tbsp	soy/rice parmesan
1 tbsp	olive oil
1½-2 tbsp	soy/rice parmesan (for topping)
1 tbsp	olive oil (optional, garnish)
2 tbsp	chives, chopped (optional, garnish)

For this 3-cup mixture, use ⅓ cup of wild rice, ½ cup brown rice, and 1¾ cups water. Rinse rice, and combine with water and a pinch of sea salt in a medium saucepan. Bring to a boil, then reduce heat to low. Cover and let simmer for 35-45 minutes, until tender. Other rice, such as basmati, can also be used.

For an even heartier entree, mix in ½ cup or more of cooked beans. For a nice crunch, top casserole with 1 cup or more of breadcrumbs, combined with the soy parmesan if you like, and a little olive oil.

Preheat oven to 375°F. In a large bowl, combine tomato paste, garlic, molasses, oregano, salt, and pepper, and mix well. Stir in remaining ingredients, except the soy parmesan for topping. (If rice is warm or hot, try to bake the dish soon after mixing to prevent overcooking some ingredients.) Transfer mixture to a lightly oiled 8"x12" baking dish and sprinkle on reserved soy parmesan. Bake for 23-27 minutes, until the top lightly browns. Remove from oven, and top with garnishes, if desired.

Makes 5-6 servings.

♥ For 6 servings (without garnishes), per serving: Calories: 206; Total Fat: 4 g (Sat. Fat: 0.5 g); Cholesterol: 0 mg; Carbohydrate: 35.2 g; Fiber: 5.2 g; Protein: 7.2 g.

Zucchini Artichoke Boats

3	*medium-large zucchini (roughly 8" long and 1½" in diameter)*
1 batch	*"Artichoke Delight Dip" (p. 58), with or without the spinach*
½ cup	*green or red peppers, chopped (or combination)*
⅓ cup	*kalamata olives, chopped*
¼ cup	*sun-dried tomatoes or red peppers, reconstituted and chopped*
¼ cup	*celery, diced*
1 cup	*good quality breadcrumbs*
	couple pinches sea salt
	couple pinches fresh ground black pepper

Preheat oven to 375°F. Trim ends off zucchini, split lengthwise, and use a spoon to scrape out seeds and some of the flesh, leaving about ¼-½" of flesh along the skin (discard scrapings). Follow directions for Artichoke Delight Dip, setting aside the ½ tbsp soy parmesan topping. Mix dip in a bowl with peppers, olives, sun-dried tomatoes, and celery. In a separate bowl, mix breadcrumbs with the reserved optional ½ tbsp soy parmesan. In an 8"x12" baking dish, place zucchini "boats" side by side to help keep them stable while baking. Distribute artichoke filling evenly in the zucchinis, heaping it on each. Sprinkle on breadcrumb topping, and a couple pinches of sea salt and pepper. Bake uncovered for 24-28 minutes until topping is lightly browned and zucchini boats are softened, but still a bit firm.

Makes 3 servings (2 "boats" each).

♥ For 6 "boats," per "boat" (without garnishes), per serving: Calories: 129; Total Fat: 4.6 g (Sat. Fat: 0.6 g); Cholesterol: 0 mg; Carbohydrate: 15.7 g; Fiber: 4.3 g; Protein: 6.6 g.

> *Using the "Artichoke Delight Dip" (p. 58), combined with tasty extras for a stuffing, zucchini is transformed into a delicious main course. You can customize the extras, using your favorite ingredients in addition to those listed (e.g., chili powder, fresh dill, green onions).*

Simple
Sides

ked Herbed Spaghetti Squash

1	medium to large spaghetti squash (about 3½-4 lbs)
	water
¼ cup	fresh parsley, chopped
¼ cup	fresh cilantro or basil, chopped
1 tbsp	olive oil
	sea salt to taste
	fresh ground black pepper to taste

Preheat oven to 400°F. Cut squash lengthwise down the center, then scoop out seeds and any stringy flesh. On a baking sheet with a raised edge, place both halves flat side down. Add ¼"-½" of water to the pan. Place pan in oven and bake for 35-40 minutes, until squash is tender when pierced and the skin is slightly browned. Using a fork, scrape out the squash flesh from the skin; it will come away in "spaghetti strands." Transfer strands into a serving bowl, and toss with fresh herbs and olive oil. Season with sea salt and black pepper to taste.
Makes 4-6 servings.

♥ For 6 servings, per serving: Calories: 115; Total Fat: 3.1 g (Sat. Fat: 0.5 g); Cholesterol: 0 mg; Carbohydrate: 19.8 g; Fiber: 4.4 g; Protein: 2.1 g.

This is wonderful served with "Sweet and Sour 'Neat' Balls" (p. 138), or in place of pasta with a very hearty pasta sauce.

Herbed Potato and Yam Fries

POTATO FRIES:

2 lbs	*all-purpose potatoes, peeling optional, cut in ½" strips*
1½-2 tbsp	*olive oil*
2 tsp	*dried oregano*
1 tsp	*dried basil*
1 tsp	*dried dill (or ½ tsp dried thyme)*
½ tsp	*onion powder (optional)*
⅛ tsp	*chili powder*
¼ tsp	*sea salt*

YAM FRIES:

3-4	*large yams (about 2 lbs), peeled, cut in ½" strips*
1½ tbsp	*olive oil*
1 tbsp	*dark soy sauce*
2 tsp	*dried basil*
1 tsp	*dried oregano*
1 tsp	*dried coriander (or more basil or oregano)*
¼ tsp	*chili powder*

These are delicious, fat-reduced fries, and the seasonings are flexible. If fat content is not a big concern, a little extra oil for the potato fries makes them even more delicious. Bake the potato and yam fries separately on baking sheets and serve together.

FOR THE POTATO FRIES:

Preheat oven to 400°F. In a large bowl, mix all ingredients. Transfer to a baking sheet lightly oiled or lined with parchment paper. Bake for 45-50 minutes, flipping after about 20 minutes, until tender and lightly browned. If also baking yam fries, rotate sheets halfway through baking. Season with additional salt and pepper if desired.

FOR THE YAM FRIES:

Same directions as above.

Both types served together will make 4-6 servings as a side dish.

♥ For 6 servings, per serving: Calories: 380; Total Fat: 8.5 g (Sat. Fat: 1.2 g); Cholesterol: 0 mg; Carbohydrate: 71 g; Fiber: 9.2 g; Protein: 5.7 g.

Lightly Sautéed Kale

1½-2 tbsp	olive oil
1-2 tbsp	shallots, minced
	sea salt to taste
	fresh ground black pepper to taste
1	good sized bunch of kale, leaves removed from stems and chopped
	olive oil (for finishing) (optional)

In a large skillet, heat olive oil over medium heat. Add shallots, season with sea salt and black pepper, and stir. Cover and sauté for 3-4 minutes until shallots start to soften. Add greens, toss with additional pinch of sea salt, and cover. Let cook for 4-6 minutes, stirring occasionally, until greens turn a bright green color and start to soften. Do not overcook, or the kale will turn a dark green-greyish color. Season to taste with additional sea salt and black pepper, and finish with a drizzle of olive oil and toss through, if desired.

Makes 3-4 servings.

♥ For 4 servings, per serving: Calories: 115; Total Fat: 7.4 g (Sat. Fat: 1 g); Cholesterol: 0 mg; Carbohydrate: 9.5 g; Fiber: 1.7 g; Protein: 2.8 g.

A wonderful and quick way to serve greens, sautéed for a few minutes to wilt slightly and bring out their vibrant color. This is a great side dish for the "Holiday Feast Menu," (p. 39) – but you may want to double the recipe for this festive dinner!

Potato "Chippers"

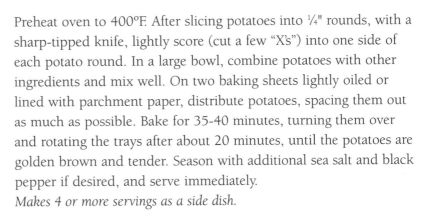

2½ lbs	*all-purpose potatoes, sliced into ¼" rounds*
2 tbsp	*olive oil*
1 tbsp	*soy parmesan (optional)*
¾ tsp	*sea salt*
½ tsp	*chili powder*
	fresh ground black pepper, to taste

Preheat oven to 400°F. After slicing potatoes into ¼" rounds, with a sharp-tipped knife, lightly score (cut a few "X's") into one side of each potato round. In a large bowl, combine potatoes with other ingredients and mix well. On two baking sheets lightly oiled or lined with parchment paper, distribute potatoes, spacing them out as much as possible. Bake for 35-40 minutes, turning them over and rotating the trays after about 20 minutes, until the potatoes are golden brown and tender. Season with additional sea salt and black pepper if desired, and serve immediately.
Makes 4 or more servings as a side dish.

♥ For 4 servings, per serving: Calories: 299; Total Fat: 7.4 g (Sat. Fat: 1 g); Cholesterol: 0 mg; Carbohydrate: 51.6 g; Fiber: 4.6 g; Protein: 6.7 g.

These are great sprinkled with a little rice vinegar, rather than white vinegar. "Mi-So Good Gravy" (p. 72) is also a great accompaniment.

Quick Asparagus Sauté

½-1 tsp   *olive oil (for sauté)*

½-¾ lb   *fresh asparagus (thinner stalks), ends trimmed*

           couple pinches sea salt

           fresh ground black pepper to taste

2-3 tsp   *fresh lemon juice*

¼-⅓ cup   *fresh cilantro, chopped*

1 tsp   *olive oil (for finishing) (optional)*

In a skillet, heat the ½-1 tsp olive oil over medium-high heat. Add asparagus, sea salt, and black pepper and sauté for 3-4 minutes, tossing often. Add lemon juice, toss again, and sauté for another couple of minutes, until asparagus has turned bright green and has seared just a little in spots (you want the asparagus to still have some crunch). Add cilantro and toss through. Remove from heat and add the 1 tsp olive oil to finish. Season further with additional sea salt and black pepper, and/or additional lemon juice, if desired. *Makes 3 servings.*

♥ For 3 servings, per serving: Calories: 62; Total Fat: 3.2 g (Sat. Fat: 0.5 g); Cholesterol: 0 mg; Carbohydrate: 5.7 g; Fiber: 2.5 g; Protein: 2.7 g.

> *Thicker asparagus will need to cook a little longer, so add a few minutes to the initial sautéing time.*

> *Substitution note: If you don't have cilantro, or aren't fond of it, you can easily substitute fresh chopped parsley, or even a couple of tablespoons of fresh chopped basil or dill.*

Quick Roast Green Beans and Peppers

¼ lb	*green beans*
1	*medium red, orange, or yellow pepper, sliced*
½-1 tsp	*olive oil*
	sea salt to taste
	fresh ground black pepper to taste
½ tsp	*balsamic vinegar*

Preheat your oven to broil. In a large bowl, combine all ingredients except balsamic vinegar and mix well. Transfer to baking sheet lightly oiled or lined with parchment paper. Broil for 5-7 minutes, until vegetables are sizzling and start to blister a little, and beans are still a bright green color. Remove from oven and transfer back to bowl. Toss with balsamic vinegar and additional sea salt and black pepper if desired. Serve immediately.
Makes 2 servings.

♥ For 2 servings, per serving: Calories: 67; Total Fat: 2.5 g (Sat. Fat: 0.3 g); Cholesterol: 0 mg; Carbohydrate: 9.5 g; Fiber: 3.5 g; Protein: 1.8 g.

This very quick, delicious side dish will serve 2 people. To make it for more, simply double or triple the recipe ingredients, depending on how many you are serving!

Roasted Baby Potatoes

1½-2 lbs	small baby or new potatoes (see sidebar)
2-3 tsp	regular or flavored olive oil
	sea salt to taste
	fresh ground black pepper to taste
	fresh rosemary, dill, or parsley, finely chopped (optional, garnish)

OPTION 1: ROASTING POTATOES WHOLE

Preheat oven to 400°F. Place whole baby potatoes on a sheet of tin foil (or baking sheet) and bake for 35-45 minutes, until very tender when pierced and skins have browned somewhat. Remove potatoes from oven, add olive oil, sea salt, and black pepper to potatoes, and toss (for easy tossing, close up tin foil around the potatoes). Keep potatoes warm in the foil until ready to serve. Sprinkle on optional herbs to finish.

Makes 3-4 servings.

OPTION 2: ROASTING POTATOES CUT INTO CHUNKS

Preheat oven to 400°F. Cut potatoes into halves or quarters, roughly 1"-1½" in size. In a large bowl, toss potatoes with olive oil, sea salt, and black pepper. Transfer to a baking dish lightly oiled or lined with parchment paper. Bake for 30-40 minutes, tossing several times, until golden and tender. Season with additional sea salt and fresh ground black pepper if desired. Sprinkle on optional herbs to finish.

Makes 3-4 servings.

♥ For 4 servings, per serving: Calories: 214; Total Fat: 3.6 g (Sat. Fat: 0.6 g); Cholesterol: 0 mg; Carbohydrate: 40.8 g; Fiber: 3.6 g; Protein: 4.7 g.

These potatoes can be done two ways for a very simple yet delicious side dish!

Substitution note: To use larger Yukon Gold or red potatoes, simply cut them into small chunks, roughly 1" in size, and follow option 2. Roasting larger potatoes whole, as in option 1, will take longer to cook, based on their size.

Serve these potatoes with "Mi-So Good Gravy" (p. 72) or "Creamy Dijon Dill Dressing" (p. 77).

Roasted Carrots and Parsnips

2-2½ cups	*carrots, sliced in diagonal rounds*
2 cups	*parsnips, sliced in diagonal rounds*
2-2½ tsp	*olive oil*
⅛-¼ tsp	*sea salt*

Preheat oven to 400°F. In a bowl, combine all ingredients and mix well to coat carrots and parsnips completely with the olive oil. Transfer to a baking dish and bake for roughly 45-50 minutes, tossing once or twice, until just fork tender (not mushy), and lightly browned in spots. Remove from oven and season further with additional sea salt and black pepper if desired.
Makes 4 or more servings.

♥ For 4 servings, per serving: Calories: 115; Total Fat: 3.2 g (Sat. Fat: 0.4 g); Cholesterol: 0 mg; Carbohydrate: 20.1 g; Fiber: 5.7 g; Protein: 1.6 g.

Roasted Fennel and Carrots with Shallots

1	large fennel bulb, cut in ¼"-½" pieces (see sidebar)
2	large carrots, sliced in rounds
¾ cup	shallots, chopped
2-2½ tsp	olive oil
⅛ tsp	sea salt
	fresh ground black pepper to taste
2-3 tbsp	fresh chopped parsley (optional)

Preheat oven to 400°F. In a bowl, combine all ingredients except fresh parsley and mix well to coat vegetables with the olive oil. Transfer to a baking sheet lightly oiled or lined with parchment paper and bake for roughly 30 minutes, turning once halfway through, until just tender and lightly browned in spots. Season further with additional sea salt and black pepper and sprinkle with optional parsley if desired.
Makes 3-4 servings.

♥ For 4 servings, per serving: Calories: 112; Total Fat: 3.1 g (Sat. Fat: 0.4 g); Cholesterol: 0 mg; Carbohydrate: 19 g; Fiber: 5.1 g; Protein: 2 g.

Use only the white, bulbous portion of the fennel; remove the green stalks and leafy portions.

Roasted Turnip Purée

Roasting turnips takes a little time but the taste is well worth it! The natural flavors and sugars are retained beneath the skin and intensify during the baking process.

◆

Another super way to roast turnips is to peel them, cut into 1" chunks, and toss with the seasonings listed. Place in a baking dish and bake covered for about 30 minutes at 400°F. Remove cover and continue baking, tossing occasionally, for about 40-50 minutes, until tender and golden brown in spots. The turnips will be caramelized with intense, earthy flavors.

◆

A "must" as part of the "Holiday Feast Menu" (p. 39), and also a great side dish for other meals, such as "Sweet and Sour 'Neat' Balls" (p. 138).

2 lbs	turnips
2-2½ tsp	olive oil
½ tsp	pure maple syrup
¼ tsp	sea salt
	few pinches cinnamon

Preheat oven to 400°F. Pierce turnips a few times and place whole on upper rack of oven, with tin foil on lower rack to catch drippings. Bake for roughly 1¾-2 hours, until turnips are very tender when pierced (baking time will vary depending on the size of turnips). Remove from oven and let cool slightly before peeling the skins. Transfer flesh to a bowl or food processor and add remaining ingredients. Using a hand blender or in the food processor, purée until smooth (you could also mash well by hand). Season with additional sea salt and black pepper if desired. Serve immediately, or return to oven on low heat to keep warm.
Makes 4 servings.

♥ For 4 servings, per serving: Calories: 94; Total Fat: 3 g (Sat. Fat: 0.4 g); Cholesterol: 0 mg; Carbohydrate: 14.7 g; Fiber: 4.1 g; Protein: 2 g.

Spicy Seared Portabella Mushrooms

1 tbsp	hoisin sauce
1 tsp	tamari or soy sauce
½ tsp	dark soy sauce (or another ½ tsp tamari)
¼-½ tsp	chipotle hot sauce (or other hot sauce)
1½ lbs	portabella mushrooms, "gills" removed, sliced into 1" pieces (see notes on cleaning mushrooms, p. 34)
½-1 tsp	olive oil
	couple pinches sea salt
	couple pinches fresh ground black pepper
1 cup	green onions (mostly green portion), cut into 1" strips

In a large bowl, mix hoisin sauce, tamari, soy sauce, and hot sauce. Add mushrooms and gently toss to coat evenly. In a large, preferably deep skillet, heat the oil on high heat and season with sea salt and black pepper. Add mushrooms and allow one side to sear for a couple of minutes, then flip to sear the other side. Add green onions and just lightly cook them. Toss mushrooms again, then remove from heat.
Makes 3-4 servings.

♥ For 4 servings, per serving: Calories: 84; Total Fat: 1.5 g (Sat. Fat: 0.3 g); Cholesterol: 0 mg; Carbohydrate: 12.5 g; Fiber: 3.4 g; Protein: 5.1 g.

Don't overcook these portabellas; they are best when they are still "meaty" and plump, with their natural juices sealed in.

Serve these mushrooms over baked yams! Bake yams in their skins until soft, then slice lengthwise and top with the mushrooms (start cooking the mushrooms once yams are already soft). The sweetness of the yams is a nice contrast to the spiciness of the mushrooms. You could also use these mushrooms in a simple fresh pasta dish (tossed with olive oil, lemon juice, and cilantro, for instance), or on top of "Parmesan Toasts" (p. 67), or to top "Savory Tofu Burgers" (p. 116).

Sweet and Simple Grain Pilaf

1-1½ tbsp	olive oil
1 tsp	mustard seeds
½ tsp	curry powder
¼ tsp	coriander powder
¼ tsp	cinnamon
⅛ tsp	ground ginger
⅛ tsp	ground cardamom
¼ tsp	sea salt
1 cup	brown rice, millet, or quinoa (see sidebar)
2 cups	water
¼ cup	raisins or currants

In a saucepan, heat oil over medium heat and add all the spices and salt. Stir and let cook for a couple of minutes, until fragrant. Add grain you are using, and stir for a minute or two. Add water and raisins, turn heat to high, and bring mixture to a boil. Reduce heat to low, cover, and let simmer for the time needed to cook the grain:

Brown rice: 45-50 minutes
Millet: 15-17 minutes
Quinoa: 8-10 minutes

Once cooked, remove from heat and serve. If you wish, drizzle in a little additional olive oil and stir to keep moist before serving. Season to taste with extra salt if desired.
Makes 4 servings.

♥ For 4 servings (using brown rice), per serving: Calories: 255; Total Fat: 6.8 g (Sat. Fat: 1 g); Cholesterol: 0 mg; Carbohydrate: 44.6 g; Fiber: 2.3 g; Protein: 4.2 g.

You can use a variety of grains in this pilaf, including brown rice, millet, and quinoa. But note the different cooking times listed depending on which grain you choose.

Tasty Tofu Tidbits

2 tbsp	*tamari or soy sauce*
2-2½ tbsp	*balsamic vinegar (see sidebar)*
	couple dashes hot sauce and/or vegan Worcestershire sauce (optional)
	couple pinches fresh ground black pepper
1	*300-g pkg extra-firm tofu, squeezed dry and cubed (see tips on preparing tofu, (p. 31)*
1-1½ tbsp	*olive oil*

In a bowl, mix tamari, balsamic vinegar, hot sauce/vegan Worcestershire sauce, and pepper. Add tofu cubes and toss, mixing well. Cover and marinate for 15 minutes, or longer, tossing once or twice (if you don't have time to marinate, just be sure the marinade distributes evenly over the cubes). In a large skillet, heat oil over medium-high heat. Add tofu and fry for roughly 4-6 minutes on at least two sides of the cubes, until browned a little and nicely seared. Serve warm or hot.
Makes 4 or more servings.

♥ For 4 servings, per serving: Calories: 172; Total Fat: 12.3 g (Sat. Fat: 1.9 g); Cholesterol: 0 mg; Carbohydrate: 3.9 g; Fiber: 0.4 g; Protein: 11.4 g.

This is a great way to enjoy morsels of tofu to serve with a stir-fry, to garnish soups, or simply as a side-dish treat! You can also mash leftover cubes with chopped veggies and an egg-free, non-dairy mayonnaise for a delicious sandwich filling.

You can replace some or all of the balsamic vinegar with rice vinegar or red wine vinegar. Also try seasoning the tofu with garlic, ginger, or dried herbs and spices such as oregano, chili powder, or cumin.

Yam Purée

2½-3 lbs	yams
2-3 tsp	olive oil
⅛-¼ tsp	fresh grated nutmeg
¼ tsp	sea salt, or more, to taste

Preheat oven to 400°F. Pierce yams a few times. Place on upper rack of oven, with a piece of tin foil on lower rack to catch drippings. Bake for 50-60 minutes, until very tender when pierced (baking times will vary based on size of yams). Remove from oven, and let cool long enough to handle. Peel skins and in a bowl or food processor, add yam flesh, olive oil, nutmeg, and sea salt. Using a hand blender or food processor, purée until smooth (you could also mash well by hand). Season with additional sea salt and pepper if desired. Serve immediately, or return to oven (on low heat) to keep warm.

Makes 4-5 servings or more.

♥ For 5 servings, per serving: Calories: 349; Total Fat: 3.2 g (Sat. Fat: 0.5 g); Cholesterol: 0 mg; Carbohydrate: 76 g; Fiber: 11.2 g; Protein: 4.2 g.

In addition to being part of the "Holiday Feast Menu" (p. 39), these yams will add taste and substance to a variety of meals. They are absolutely delicious as the base for a stir-fry, or as an alternative to rice or couscous. Think about having them in a meal where you might otherwise have mashed potatoes: a great change from the old standby!

Muffins
and Snack Loaves

Notes for Muffins, Snack Loaves, and Sweet Treats

1. I avoid using refined sugar whenever possible. Refined sugars (including white granulated sugar, icing sugar, brown sugar, and corn syrup) are nutritionally deficient, and stressful to your digestive system. I also never use artificial sweeteners (such as aspartame or saccharin). My recipes use sweeteners such as pure maple syrup, molasses, unrefined sugar, and occasionally stevia (which is given as an option in a Sweet Treat recipe).

2. Similarly, I minimize the amount of white flour in many of these recipes, because it is nutritionally weak, and more difficult for your body to digest than other flours. Instead I use whole wheat flour, kamut flour, and rolled oats ground into a "flour." For many of the Sweet Treat recipes, white flour really is important for the taste and texture of these desserts, and so is used either in part or in full – for special desserts, it is worth it!

3. Canola oil is used for the fat component in these recipes. I never use hydrogenated or partially hydrogenated oils, as found in most margarines.

4. A little bit of salt is added to most recipes. In general, a couple pinches of salt is important for baked goods and dessert recipes, as it heightens the flavors and sweetness of the other ingredients.

Apple Swirl Loaf

APPLE MIXTURE:

½ cup	apple, cored, peeled, and diced
1 tsp	lemon juice
¼ cup	unsweetened applesauce
¼ cup	unrefined sugar
1 tsp	cinnamon
⅛ tsp	allspice

BATTER:

1½ cup	whole wheat pastry flour (or ¾ cup each whole wheat flour and unbleached all-purpose flour)
½ cup	ground oats (see sidebar)
1½ tsp	baking powder
½ tsp	baking soda
½ tsp	cinnamon
	couple pinches sea salt
¾ cup	vanilla or plain soy milk
½ cup	pure maple syrup
2 tsp	pure vanilla extract
1 tbsp	canola oil

Use a food processor to grind the oats. I use "quick oats" and process them until the consistency is close to a coarse flour.

Preheat oven to 350°F. In a bowl, toss apples with lemon juice, then add remaining apple mixture ingredients, mix, and set aside. In a large bowl, combine dry ingredients, sifting in baking powder and baking soda. Mix well. In another bowl, combine soy milk, maple syrup, and vanilla. Add this wet mixture to dry mixture. Mix until just combined, then stir in canola oil, again until just mixed. Add apple mixture to batter, using a knife to swirl it lightly into the batter (don't mix through, just swirl in a little). Pour into a lightly oiled 9"x5" loaf pan. Bake for 43-45 minutes, until golden brown and a toothpick inserted in the center comes out clean.

♥ For 10 loaf slices, per slice: Calories: 170; Total Fat: 2.4 g (Sat. Fat: 0.1 g); Cholesterol: 0 mg; Carbohydrate: 34.2 g; Fiber: 2.4 g; Protein: 3.4 g.

As-You-Like Muffins

1 cup	whole wheat pastry flour (or ½ cup each of whole wheat flour and unbleached all-purpose flour)
1 cup	ground oats (see sidebar)
1½ tsp	baking powder
½ tsp	baking soda
¼-½ tsp	cinnamon
½-¾ cup	fruit or nuts (see sidebar)
¼ cup	unrefined sugar
	couple pinches sea salt
1 cup	unsweetened applesauce
½ cup	vanilla or plain soy milk
¼ cup	pure maple syrup
2 tsp	pure vanilla extract
1 tbsp	canola oil

Preheat oven to 375°F. In a large bowl, combine flour and ground oats. Sift in baking powder, baking soda, and cinnamon, then stir in remaining dry ingredients (including fruit or nuts), and combine well. In another bowl, mix applesauce, soy milk, maple syrup, and vanilla, and add this to the dry mixture. Stir and add canola oil as it starts to come together. Mix until just combined (do not overmix). Spoon into a lined or lightly oiled muffin pan and bake for 19-24 minutes, until golden brown and a toothpick inserted in the center comes out clean.

Makes 9-10 medium to large muffins.

♥ For 10 muffins, per muffin: Calories: 174; Total Fat: 2.4 g (Sat. Fat: 0.2 g); Cholesterol: 0 mg; Carbohydrate: 35.2 g; Fiber: 3.1 g; Protein: 3.1 g.

Use a food processor to grind the oats. I use "quick oats" and process them until the consistency is close to a coarse flour.

This light and fluffy muffin batter can be varied to include your favorite fruit or nuts.

Here are some tasty variations:
Cran-Date Muffins:
½ cup dried cranberries and ¼ cup chopped dates
Chocolate Chip Muffins:
½-¾ cup chocolate or carob chips
Raisin Nut Muffins:
½ cup raisins and ¼ cup toasted pecans or walnuts
Tropical Muffins:
¼ cup each chopped dried pineapple, apricots, and shredded coconut, and ½-1 tsp coconut extract to replace some vanilla

Carrot Pineapple Muffins
(or "Tops")

2 cups	whole wheat pastry flour (or 1 cup each whole wheat flour and unbleached all-purpose flour)
¼ cup	unrefined sugar
1½ tsp	baking powder
½ tsp	baking soda
½ tsp	fresh nutmeg, grated
1½ tsp	cinnamon
	couple pinches sea salt
¾ cup	carrots, finely grated
1	8-oz can crushed pineapple, well drained (roughly ½ cup)
¼ cup	raisins
¼ cup	pure maple syrup
1 cup + 2 tbsp vanilla or plain soy milk	
1 tsp	pure vanilla extract
2 tbsp	canola oil

For making muffin "tops," place large scoops of the mixture on two baking sheets lightly oiled or lined with parchment paper (about 5-6 per sheet). Bake for 18-20 minutes, rotating the sheets between upper and lower rack once halfway through, until "tops" are golden brown and a toothpick inserted comes out clean. For better results, bake sheets separately. This will make 10-12 "tops."

Add 3-4 tbsp chopped toasted pecans or walnuts to this batter for added flavor and texture.

Preheat oven to 375°F. In a large bowl, combine dry ingredients, sifting in baking soda and baking powder. Mix well. Add carrots, pineapple, and raisins, and stir well. In a separate bowl, combine maple syrup, soy milk, and vanilla, and add to dry mixture. Stir through, and as it starts to come together, add canola oil, and stir until mixture is just combined. Spoon into a lined or lightly oiled muffin pan and bake for 19-23 minutes until golden brown and a toothpick inserted in the center comes out clean.
Makes 10-12 muffins.

♥ For 12 muffins, per muffin: Calories: 156; Total Fat: 3 g (Sat. Fat: 0.2 g); Cholesterol: 0 mg; Carbohydrate: 28.9 g; Fiber: 2.4 g; Protein: 3.4 g.

Cinnamon Cornmeal Muffins

½ cup	vanilla soy milk
½ cup	fine cornmeal
1 cup	whole wheat or whole wheat pastry flour
½ cup	Kamut flour (or other flour, see sidebar)
2 tsp	cinnamon
1½ tsp	baking powder
½ tsp	baking soda
	couple pinches sea salt
½ cup	pure maple syrup
½ cup	unsweetened applesauce
1 tsp	pure vanilla extract
1½ tbsp	canola oil

Preheat oven to 375°F. In a medium bowl, combine soy milk and cornmeal to soak while you prepare the other ingredients. In a large bowl, combine all other dry ingredients, sifting in baking powder and baking soda. Mix well. To the soy milk/cornmeal mixture, add maple syrup, applesauce, and vanilla extract. Mix together well, then add to dry mixture. Stir through and add canola oil just as mixture starts to come together. Spoon into a lined or lightly oiled muffin pan (roughly ¾ full) and bake for 16-19 minutes, until golden brown and a toothpick inserted in the center comes out clean.

Makes 8-9 muffins.

♥ For 9 muffins (using whole wheat flour), per muffin: Calories: 177; Total Fat: 3.1 g (Sat. Fat: 0.2 g); Cholesterol: 0 mg; Carbohydrate: 33.9 g; Fiber: 3.6 g; Protein: 3.7 g.

Kamut flour adds a nice texture to this recipe, but if you don't have it, you can use unbleached all-purpose flour or more whole wheat flour. When using whole wheat flour, the muffins bake faster than with the Kamut flour combination. Whatever combination you choose, at 16 minutes check your muffins for "doneness" so they don't dry out.

Maple Banana Loaf

¾ cup	whole wheat pastry flour
1 cup	Kamut or more whole wheat pastry flour (see sidebar)
2 tsp	baking powder
½ tsp	baking soda
1 tsp	cinnamon
½ tsp	fresh nutmeg, grated
	couple pinches sea salt
1 cup	very ripe banana, mashed
½ cup	pure maple syrup
½ cup	vanilla or plain soy milk
1 tsp	pure vanilla extract
1 tbsp	canola oil

If using more whole wheat pastry flour instead of Kamut, you may need a couple of extra tablespoons of soy milk to lighten the batter.

For a little decadence, try ¼ cup of non-dairy chocolate chips (add in with the dry ingredients). Also try adding ¼ cup toasted nuts, such as pecans or walnuts.

Preheat oven to 350°F. In a large bowl, combine dry ingredients, sifting in baking powder and baking soda. Mix well. In a separate bowl, combine mashed banana with maple syrup, soy milk, and vanilla extract. Mix well, then add to dry mixture. Stir through and add canola oil just as mixture starts to come together. Mix until just combined (do not overmix). Pour into a lightly oiled 9"x5" loaf pan and bake for 45-50 minutes, until golden brown and a toothpick inserted in the center comes out clean.

♥ For 10 slices of loaf (using only whole wheat pastry flour), per slice: Calories: 161; Total Fat: 2 g (Sat. Fat: 0.1 g); Cholesterol: 0 mg; Carbohydrate: 32.8 g; Fiber: 2.2 g; Protein: 3 g.

Orange Almond "Scones"

1 cup	ground oats (see sidebar)
1 cup	whole wheat pastry or whole wheat flour
1½ tsp	baking powder
½ tsp	baking soda
¼ cup	unrefined sugar
½ tsp	fresh nutmeg, grated
	couple pinches sea salt
2 tbsp	almond pieces, toasted (can use other nuts; for tips on toasting nuts, see p. 36)
½ cup	vanilla or plain soy milk
⅓ cup	orange juice, fresh squeezed, or good quality
1-2 tbsp	honey option (for notes on honey options, see p. 29)
1 tsp	orange zest (zest of roughly 1 orange)
½-1 tsp	almond extract
2 tbsp	canola oil

Use a food processor to grind the oats. I use "quick oats" and process them until the consistency is close to a coarse flour.

Preheat oven to 350°F. In a large bowl combine ground oats with whole wheat pastry flour. Sift in baking powder and baking soda, then stir in remaining dry ingredients, and mix well. In a separate bowl, combine soy milk, orange juice, honey alternative, orange zest, and almond extract. Mix well, then add to dry mixture. Stir through and add canola oil just as mixture starts to come together. Mix until just well combined. Scoop large spoonfuls of the mixture (roughly ½ cup each) and place onto a baking sheet lined with parchment paper or lightly oiled. Bake for 16-18 minutes, until the scones start to turn golden brown and a toothpick inserted in the center comes out clean.

Makes 6 scones.

♥ For 6 scones (using whole wheat flour), per scone: Calories: 251; Total Fat: 7.2 g (Sat. Fat: 0.7 g); Cholesterol: 0 mg; Carbohydrate: 40.2 g; Fiber: 4.3 g; Protein: 6 g.

Pumpkin Raisin Loaf

1 cup	whole wheat pastry flour
1 cup	Kamut flour
¼ cup	unrefined sugar
2 tsp	baking powder
½ tsp	baking soda
1½ tsp	cinnamon
½ tsp	fresh nutmeg, grated
½ tsp	allspice
	couple pinches sea salt
1 cup	canned pumpkin (see sidebar)
1 cup	vanilla or plain soy milk
⅓ cup	pure maple syrup
¼-⅓ cup	raisins
1 tsp	pure vanilla extract
2 tbsp	canola oil

The consistency and moisture of canned pumpkin can vary quite a bit, so the thickness of your batter and baking time may change from one loaf to the next.

◆

Try adding 3-4 tbsp of your favorite toasted nuts for more flavor, and a little crunch!

Preheat oven to 350°F. In a large bowl, combine dry ingredients, sifting in baking powder and baking soda, and mix well. In a separate bowl, combine pumpkin, soy milk, maple syrup, raisins, and vanilla extract. Mix well, then add to dry mixture. Stir through and add canola oil just as mixture starts to come together. If your batter is very thick, add a little extra soy milk (see sidebar). Pour into a lightly oiled 9"x5" loaf pan and bake for 45-55 minutes, until a toothpick inserted in the center comes out clean.

♥ For 10 slices (using only whole wheat flour), per slice: Calories: 201; Total Fat: 3.6 g (Sat. Fat: 0.3 g); Cholesterol: 0 mg; Carbohydrate: 37.8 g; Fiber: 3.2 g; Protein: 4.1 g.

Sweet Treats

Almond Whipped "Cream"

1	*300-g pkg almond dessert or dessert tofu*
½ cup	*vanilla soy milk*
2½-3 tbsp	*arrowroot flour*
1-2 tbsp	*unrefined sugar or maple syrup*
	couple pinches sea salt
½ tsp	*pure vanilla extract*
¼ tsp	*almond extract*
¼ tsp	*orange zest (optional)*

In a food processor and using a hand blender, combine tofu, soy milk, arrowroot, sugar/maple syrup, and salt, and purée until very smooth. Transfer to a saucepan over medium heat. Stirring frequently, bring mixture to a very thick consistency, and just before it comes to a boil, remove from heat (otherwise mixture may turn sticky and gummy, particularly once it has cooled). Stir in vanilla and almond extracts, and optional orange zest. Let cool, covered, then transfer to a covered bowl or container to chill in the refrigerator.

Makes 4-5 servings.

♥ For 5 servings (using almond dessert tofu), per serving: Calories: 85; Total Fat: 1.3 g (Sat. Fat: 0.2 g); Cholesterol: 0 mg; Carbohydrate: 16.1 g; Fiber: n/a; Protein: 2.4 g.

I have experimented using stevia as the sweetener for this recipe. If you would like to try it, use a few pinches in place of the 2 tbsp sugar. Check the sweetness to taste, and adjust with just a pinch of stevia each time, as it is very sweet and can be overpowering. (For notes on stevia, see p. 30.)

Banana Ice "Cream"

This is a delicious, low-fat, creamy treat that always gets a smile! Best of all, you can easily adjust flavorings to your preference.

◆

You can use plain soy milk instead of vanilla, but vanilla is preferable, Also, use a good quality soy milk that may be a little higher in fat; it will give a "creamier" texture and taste.

◆

Try other favorite extracts in place of coconut, such as butterscotch, rum, and almond. For a "chocolatey" treat, replace the nutmeg, cinnamon, maple syrup, coconut extract, with ½ cup chocolate syrup (or more, to taste); also try adding ¼ cup chocolate chips and purée just a little (so still a little chunky). If nuts are your thing, stir in some of your favorite nuts after puréeing. If you pre-toast the nuts, their flavor will be enhanced.

3½-4 cups	*frozen, overripe banana, cut in chunks (about 4 medium bananas)*
⅓ cup	*pure maple syrup*
1 tsp.	*pure vanilla extract*
½ tsp.	*coconut extract (optional, see sidebar)*
¼ tsp.	*cinnamon*
¼ tsp.	*fresh grated nutmeg*
⅓-½ cup	*vanilla or plain soy milk (see sidebar)*

In a food processor, purée frozen bananas, pulsing several times, and scraping the sides of the bowl in between. When the mixture thickens and becomes difficult to blend, add the maple syrup and extracts and blend again. As the mixture fluffs and becomes smooth, add cinnamon and nutmeg and blend again. Add soy milk to desired consistency and taste; you may not need to use all of it. When consistency is similar to that of soft-serve ice-cream or frozen yogurt, it is ready to serve. This can be put in the freezer, but if left for an hour or more, it will get quite hard. To soften, simply thaw a little, or reblend with additional soy milk.
Makes 3-4 servings.

♥ For 4 servings, per serving: Calories: 313; Total Fat: 1.9 g (Sat. Fat: 0.5 g); Cholesterol: 0 mg; Carbohydrate: 71.3 g; Fiber: 5.9 g; Protein: 3.1 g.

Blueberry Ice "Cream"

1	300-g pkg dessert or almond dessert tofu
¼ cup	pure maple syrup
1 tsp	pure vanilla extract
¾ cup	frozen, overripe banana, cut in chunks
2 cups	frozen blueberries

In a food processor, combine tofu, maple syrup, and vanilla extract, and mix well, scraping down the sides of the bowl. Add frozen banana, and purée until just smooth. Add blueberries and blend to desired consistency. This can be put in the freezer, but if left for an hour or more, it will get quite hard. To soften, simply thaw a little, or reblend with additional soy milk.
Makes 3-4 servings.

♥ For 4 servings, per serving: Calories: 192; Total Fat: 2.1 g (Sat. Fat: 0.3 g); Cholesterol: 0 mg; Carbohydrate: 40.8 g; Fiber: n/a; Protein: 2.8 g.

Other frozen berries or fruit can be used to replace some or all of the blueberries, including raspberries, strawberries, or peaches. You may need to adjust the sweetener, depending on the fruits used.

EVAN-illa Rice Pudding

½ cup	arborio rice
1 cup	water
3 cups	vanilla soy milk (use 2½ cups first, and then remaining ½ cup) (see sidebar)
½ cup	unrefined sugar
⅓ cup	raisins (optional, see sidebar)
¼ tsp	fresh nutmeg, grated
	couple pinches sea salt
1 tbsp	arrowroot flour
1 tsp	pure vanilla extract

My nephew Evan loves this pudding, and us "big kids" love it too! It's low in fat, yet is deliciously creamy and thick, thanks to the arborio rice and a good quality vanilla soy milk.

You can use plain soy milk instead of vanilla, but vanilla is preferable. Also, use a good quality soy milk that may be a little higher in fat for best results. Fat-free soy milk may make the pudding somewhat watery.

Experiment with other dried fruit, such as dried cherries or cranberries, instead of, or in addition to, the raisins: a customized comfort snack!

Rinse rice, then transfer to a medium-large saucepan with water. Bring to a boil, then reduce heat to low. Cover and cook rice for 12-13 minutes. Add 2½ cups soy milk, sugar, raisins, nutmeg, and salt. In a bowl, combine remaining ½ cup soy milk with arrowroot flour until well dissolved. Add to saucepan, bring mixture to a boil, then immediately reduce the heat to very low to allow the boiling to come down. Cover and cook on low for about 40 minutes, stirring every 10-15 minutes. (If it starts to boil over, remove cover for a few minutes, then re-cover). Remove cover to let mixture reduce and finish, for roughly 8-10 minutes. Stir frequently to prevent a skin from developing on the top (if a little does, stir it through). Pudding should be nicely thickened, and will thicken more once chilled. Remove pudding from heat and stir in the vanilla extract. Cover and let cool a little before serving. *Makes 4 or more servings.*

♥ For 4 servings, per serving: Calories: 302; Total Fat: 3.8 g (Sat. Fat: 0.4 g); Cholesterol: 0 mg; Carbohydrate: 59.9 g; Fiber: 4.1 g; Protein: 7 g.

Hot Fudge Sauce

⅓ cup   *cocoa powder*

½ cup + 2 tbsp *vanilla or plain soy milk*

½ cup   *unrefined sugar*

           few pinches sea salt

2 tbsp   *(generous) non-dairy chocolate chips*

1 tsp   *pure vanilla extract*

In a blender or using a hand blender, combine cocoa powder, soy milk, sugar, and sea salt, and purée until smooth. Transfer mixture to a saucepan over medium heat, add chocolate chips, and stir through. Turn the heat to medium high, and continue to stir until mixture just starts to reach a slow boil. Remove from heat (do not let it boil as it can burn). Stir in vanilla extract, and serve (see sidebar).

Makes roughly 1¼ cups.

♥ For ¹⁄₁₀ of sauce (roughly 2 tbsp), per serving: Calories: 73; Total Fat: 1.5 g (Sat. Fat: 0.7 g); Cholesterol: 0 mg; Carbohydrate: 13.7 g; Fiber: 1.3 g; Protein: 1.3 g.

You can serve this sauce hot, warm, or cold, but note that it will thicken as it cools.

Mango Ice "Cream"

½ cup	*frozen overripe banana, cut in chunks*
3	*frozen ripe mangoes, peeled, pitted, chopped (roughly 2½-3 cups)*
1 tsp	*pure vanilla extract*
½-¾ cup	*vanilla soy milk*
2-4 tbsp	*maple syrup (see sidebar)*

In a food processor, process chopped banana until it begins to smooth out. Add mangoes and vanilla extract, and purée, scraping down the sides of the bowl. Add soy milk (start with ½ cup), and blend until very smooth, adding more if mixture is too thick or is not smoothing out. Check sweetness, and adjust to taste with maple syrup. Serve, or put in the freezer. Freezing the mixture for an hour or more will harden it. To soften, simply thaw a little, or reblend with additional soy milk.
Makes 3-4 servings.

♥ For 4 servings, per serving: Calories: 188; Total Fat: 1.3 g (Sat. Fat: 0.3 g); Cholesterol: 0 mg; Carbohydrate: 41.7 g; Fiber: 3.5 g; Protein: 2.2 g.

Adjust the amount of maple syrup you use based on the sweetness of your mangoes. You can also substitute another liquid sweetener, if you prefer.

Tropical Rice Pudding

½ cup	arborio rice
1 cup	water
1½ cups	low-fat coconut milk (not quite a 398-ml can)
1½ cups	vanilla or plain soy milk
½ cup	unrefined sugar
¼ cup	unsweetened shredded coconut
2 tbsp	dried pineapple or apricots, finely chopped
¼ tsp	fresh nutmeg, grated
	couple pinches sea salt
1 tbsp	arrowroot flour
½-¾ tsp	coconut extract

Rinse rice, and place in a medium-large saucepan with water. Bring to a boil, then reduce heat to low. Cover and cook for 12-13 minutes. Add the coconut milk, 1 cup soy milk, sugar, coconut, pineapple, nutmeg, and salt. In remaining ½ cup soy milk, mix in arrowroot flour until well dissolved. Add this to the saucepan and bring mixture to a boil, then immediately reduce the heat to very low. Cover and simmer for roughly 40 minutes, stirring every 10-15 minutes. Then remove cover to let mixture reduce and finish, for 8-10 minutes, stirring frequently to prevent a skin from developing on the surface (if a little does, stir it through). Pudding should be nicely thickened, and will thicken more once chilled. Remove from heat and stir in coconut extract. Cover and cool a little before serving.
Makes 4 or more servings.

♥ For 4 servings, per serving: Calories: 332; Total Fat: 10.3 g (Sat. Fat: 6.5 g); Cholesterol: 0 mg; Carbohydrate: 55.2 g; Fiber: 3.3 g; Protein: 5 g.

This pudding is similar to "EVAN-illa Rice Pudding" (p. 175), but with tropical flavors, and a creamier and richer texture thanks to the low-fat coconut milk! This version is not as sweet, however, since half the soy milk is replaced with coconut milk. If you want it sweeter, add a little extra unrefined sugar while cooking, or stir in some maple syrup once done, adjusting to taste.

Substitution Idea: In place of, or in addition to, the dried pineapple or apricots, try dried papaya, mango, or any combination thereof!

"Bill-Friendly" Cookies

1 cup	ground oats (see sidebar)
2 tbsp	toasted pecans (for tips on toasting nuts, see p. 36)
2 tbsp	unbleached all-purpose flour
½ tsp	cinnamon
¼ tsp	fresh nutmeg, grated
	pinch powdered stevia extract (optional; see sidebar)
	couple pinches sea salt
⅓ cup + 2 tbsp raisins (see sidebar)	
⅓ cup	orange juice, fresh squeezed or good quality
1 tsp	pure vanilla extract
½ tsp	almond extract
3 tbsp	canola oil

My friend Bill avoids sugars in his diet, and so when I make desserts he often asks, "Are they Bill-friendly?" These definitely are! They're sweetened with a purée of raisins and orange juice. I also use stevia, but just a pinch, it can be very overpowering. Alternatively, you can add a few tsp unrefined sugar or maple syrup.

◆

Use a food processor to grind the oats. I use "quick oats" and process them until the consistency is close to a coarse flour.

◆

These cookies are also good with a couple of tbsp dried cranberries. Other dried fruit could also be used in place of, or in addition to, the 2 tbsp raisins.

Preheat oven to 350°F. In a bowl, combine ground oats, pecans, flour, cinnamon, nutmeg, optional stevia, and sea salt, and mix well. In a blender or food processor, purée the ⅓ cup raisins, orange juice, and vanilla and almond extracts. Add this wet mixture to dry mixture, as well as the other 2 tbsp raisins, and mix together, adding canola oil as it starts to come together. Take spoonfuls of mixture and form into balls, lightly flatten out and place on a baking sheet lightly oiled or lined with parchment paper. Bake for 14-16 minutes.
Makes 11-12 cookies.

♥ For 12 cookies, per cookie: Calories: 94; Total Fat: 4.6 g (Sat. Fat: 0.4 g); Cholesterol: 0 mg; Carbohydrate: 11.4 g; Fiber: 1.3 g; Protein: 1.4 g.

Chewy Nutty Cereal Chip Squares

½ cup	almond butter (see sidebar)
3 tbsp	honey option (for notes on honey options, see p. 29)
2 tbsp	pure maple syrup
1 tbsp	vanilla or plain soy milk
	couple pinches sea salt
1 tsp	pure vanilla extract
3 tbsp	shredded coconut
2 cups	rice crisp cereal
2-3 tbsp	non-dairy chocolate chips (see sidebar)

In a saucepan over medium-low heat, combine almond butter, honey option, maple syrup, soy milk, and salt. Heat mixture slowly until just well melted, about 4-5 minutes (careful not to boil). Remove from heat and stir in vanilla, coconut, rice crisp cereal, and chocolate chips (add chips last because they will melt too quickly if added sooner). Spoon mixture into a lightly oiled 8"x8" baking pan, then press mixture down evenly. Refrigerate until cool, then cut into squares.
Makes 12-16 squares.

♥ For 16 squares, per square: Calories: 108; Total Fat: 5.7 g (Sat. Fat: 1.1 g); Cholesterol: 0 mg; Carbohydrate: 12.1 g; Fiber: 0.5 g; Protein: 1.6 g.

Substitution idea: Instead of almond butter, try another natural nut butter, such as peanut or cashew. And instead of chocolate chips, try adding raisins or toasted chopped nuts, such as almonds.

Coconut-Pineapple-Carrot Macaroons

1 cup	unsweetened shredded coconut
1¼ cup	ground oats (see sidebar)
¼ cup + 2 tbsp unrefined sugar	
	couple pinches sea salt
1 tsp	baking powder
1	8-oz/227-ml can unsweetened crushed pineapple, lightly drained
½ cup	carrots, finely grated
¼ cup	vanilla or plain soy milk
1 tsp	pure vanilla extract
¼ tsp	coconut extract
1½ tbsp	canola oil

Preheat oven to 350°F. In a bowl, combine shredded coconut, ground oats, sugar, and salt, and sift in baking powder. Stir to mix well, then add pineapple, carrot, soy milk, and vanilla and coconut extracts, and stir through. As mixture starts to come together, add in canola oil and stir until just combined. Spoon mounds (do not flatten) onto a baking sheet lightly oiled or lined with parchment paper. Bake for 18-20 minutes, until cookies are golden brown in spots. Remove from oven, cool for a couple of minutes on the pan, then transfer to a cooling rack.

Makes 15-16 medium to large macaroons.

♥ For 16 cookies, per cookie: Calories: 109; Total Fat: 5.6 g (Sat. Fat: 3.5 g); Cholesterol: 0 mg; Carbohydrate: 13.1 g; Fiber: 1.8 g; Protein: 1.6 g.

Use a food processor to grind the oats. I use "quick oats" and process them until the consistency is close to a coarse flour.

These are best after they've cooled a little out of the oven. Once you store them in a container, or freeze them, they lose their outside crispiness, which contrasts nicely with the moist center.

Coconut Raspberry Squares

BOTTOM LAYER:

1¼ cup	unsweetened shredded coconut
½ cup	unbleached all-purpose flour
2 tbsp	unrefined sugar
	few pinches sea salt
¼ cup	vanilla or plain soy milk
¼ cup	pure maple syrup
¼-½ tsp	coconut extract
¼ tsp	pure vanilla extract
2 tbsp	canola oil

FILLING:

½ cup + 2-3 tbsp raspberry jam (see sidebar)

TOPPING:

½ cup	unsweetened shredded coconut
¼ cup	unbleached all-purpose flour
	pinch sea salt
1½ tbsp	canola oil

You can substitute other flavors of jam if you like, such as strawberry or a field berry blend. I love the raspberry flavor in this recipe, and these squares have become a family favorite!

Preheat oven to 350°F. For the bottom layer, mix dry ingredients together first. Then combine soy milk, maple syrup, and coconut and vanilla extracts, and mix into dry ingredients, then add canola oil, stirring until just well combined (the mixture will be fairly thick). Spoon mixture into a lightly oiled 8"x8" baking pan. Spread raspberry jam over this layer. In another bowl, combine topping ingredients, and work into a crumbly mixture with your hands. Sprinkle this topping over the raspberry jam. Bake for 28-30 minutes, until topping is a light golden brown and jam is bubbling a little. Remove from oven, and let cool before cutting into pieces. *Makes 12-16 squares.*

♥ For 16 squares, per square: Calories: 175; Total Fat: 9.7 g (Sat. Fat: 6.1 g); Cholesterol: 0 mg; Carbohydrate: 20.7 g; Fiber: 2 g; Protein: 1.5 g.

Double Chocolate Pecan Chippers

¼ cup	unbleached all-purpose flour
¼ cup	cocoa powder
½ tsp	baking soda
¾ cup	unrefined sugar (see sidebar)
½ cup	ground oats (see sidebar)
¼ cup	quick oats
⅓ cup	non-dairy chocolate chips (or more, if you like!)
¼ cup	toasted pecans (for tips on toasting nuts, see p. 36)
	few pinches sea salt
¼ cup	water
1 tsp	pure vanilla extract
½ tsp	mocha or almond extract (or more vanilla)
3 tbsp	canola oil

Use a food processor to grind the oats. I use "quick oats" and process them until the consistency is close to a coarse flour.

You can use cane juice sugar, but the cookies will not be quite as crispy. The unrefined sugar I use is similar to white sugar in appearance, but with larger granules and golden in color.

Preheat oven to 350°F. In a bowl, sift flour with cocoa powder and baking soda. Mix in remaining dry ingredients until well combined. Stir in water, and vanilla and mocha extracts. Add in canola oil as batter is coming together, and mix until well combined. If possible, chill the batter, as it will be less sticky and easier to form. Take spoonfuls of batter (about 1 tbsp each) and form into balls. Place onto a large baking sheet lightly oiled or lined with parchment paper. Space cookies out as much as possible. Bake for 13-15 minutes, being careful not to overbake or they will dry out. Remove from oven and let cool on the pan for a few minutes (again, not too long or they will dry out) before transferring to a cooling rack. (Note that the cookies will flatten while baking and may join at the edges. If so, separate them with a spatula or knife before transferring to rack.)
Makes 22-24 cookies.

♥ For 24 cookies, per cookie: Calories: 86; Total Fat: 3.8 g (Sat. Fat: 0.9 g); Cholesterol: 0 mg; Carbohydrate: 11.8 g; Fiber: 1 g; Protein: 1.1 g.

Hint O' Cinnamon
Chocolate Chippers

¼ cup	unbleached all-purpose flour
½ tsp	baking soda
1 cup	ground oats (see sidebar)
¾ cup	unrefined sugar (see sidebar)
⅓ cup	non-dairy chocolate chips (or more, if you like!)
¼ tsp	cinnamon
	few pinches of sea salt
¼ cup	water
2 tsp	pure vanilla extract
3 tbsp	canola oil (a scant 3 tbsp)

Preheat oven to 350°F. In a bowl, sift together flour and baking soda. Add remaining dry ingredients and stir until mixed well. Add water and vanilla and mix through. Add canola oil as batter is coming together, and mix until well combined. Chill batter if possible, as it will be less sticky and easier to form. Take spoonfuls of batter (about 1 tbsp each) and form into balls. Place onto a large baking sheet lightly oiled or lined with parchment paper. Space cookies out as much as possible. Bake for 13-15 minutes, being careful not to overbake or they will dry out. Remove from oven and let cool on the pan for a couple of minutes (again, not too long or they will dry out) before transferring to a cooling rack. (Note that the cookies will flatten while baking and may join at the edges. If so, separate them with a spatula or knife before transferring them to rack.)
Makes 22-24 cookies.

♥ For 24 cookies, per cookie: Calories: 76; Total Fat: 2.9 g (Sat. Fat: 0.7 g); Cholesterol: 0 mg; Carbohydrate: 11.7 g; Fiber: 0.7 g; Protein: 0.9 g.

Use a food processor to grind the oats. I use "quick oats" and process them until the consistency is close to a coarse flour.

You can use cane juice sugar, but the cookies will not be quite as crispy. The unrefined sugar I use is similar to white sugar in appearance, but with larger granules and golden in color.

Try adding a few tbsp of toasted chopped nuts to the batter, such as almonds, pecans, or walnuts ... delicious!

Marie's "More-ish" Brownies

¾ cup	unbleached all-purpose flour (see sidebar)
½ cup	cocoa powder
½ tsp	baking soda
¾ cup	unrefined sugar
¼ tsp	sea salt
½ cup	soft tofu
½ cup + 2 tbsp water	
1 tsp	pure vanilla extract
2 tbsp	ground flax meal
¾ cup	non-dairy chocolate chips
2 tbsp	(generous) canola oil
¼ cup	non-dairy chocolate chips, crushed

Preheat oven to 375°F. In a bowl, sift together flour, cocoa powder, and baking soda. Stir in sugar and salt, and mix well. In a food processor or with a hand blender, combine tofu, water, vanilla, and flax meal, and purée until very smooth. In a pot over boiling water, melt the ¾ cup chocolate chips (for tips on melting chocolate, see p. 36). Add melted chocolate to tofu mixture and purée until completely smooth, scraping down the sides of the bowl a couple of times. Stir this mixture into dry mixture. Add canola oil just as it comes together, mixing until just well combined. Pour batter into a lightly oiled 8"x8" baking pan (see sidebar). Sprinkle on ¼ cup crushed chocolate chips, and press lightly into batter. Bake for 30-35 minutes (longer for firmer brownies, and shorter for softer "gooier" ones). Remove from oven and let cool in pan. For best results, chill the brownies in the refrigerator before cutting.
Makes 12-16 brownies.

♥ For 16 brownies, per brownie: Calories: 182; Total Fat: 7.3 g (Sat. Fat: 3.1 g); Cholesterol: 0 mg; Carbohydrate: 26.4 g; Fiber: 2.6 g; Protein: 3 g.

My mother uses the term "more-ish" to describe foods that entice you back for more. These brownies are just that, so moist and "chocolatey" … try to eat just one, Mom!

I occasionally like to substitute some Kamut flour for the white, between ¼-½ cup. It is healthier than white flour, and it also adds some texture.

These brownies are thick, but if you want more shallow brownies, you can divide the batter between two pans. The baking time will reduce to roughly 24-27 minutes.

Try adding ¼ cup toasted nuts, or for "Black Forest" brownies, add some dried cherries.

Oatmeal Raisin Cookies

1 cup	*ground oats (see sidebar)*
¼ cup	*rolled oats*
¼ cup	*unbleached all-purpose flour*
¾ cup	*unrefined sugar (see sidebar)*
¼-⅓ cup	*raisins*
½ tsp	*baking soda*
¾ tsp	*cinnamon*
¼ tsp	*fresh nutmeg, grated*
	few pinches sea salt
¼ cup	*water*
2 tsp	*pure vanilla extract*
3 tbsp	*canola oil*

Preheat oven to 350°F. In a bowl, sift together flour and baking soda, then add in remaining dry ingredients. Mix well. Add water and vanilla and mix through. Add canola oil as batter is coming together, and mix until well combined. Chill batter if possible, as it will be less sticky and easier to form. Take spoonfuls of batter (roughly 1 tbsp each) and form into balls. Place onto a large baking sheet lightly oiled or lined with parchment paper. Space cookies out as much as possible. Bake for 13-15 minutes, being careful not to overbake or they will dry out. Remove from oven and let cool on the pan for a few minutes (again, not too long, or they will dry out) before transferring to a cooling rack. (Note that cookies will flatten while baking and may join at the edges. If so, separate them with a spatula or knife before transferring them to rack.)
Makes 22-24 cookies.

♥ For 24 cookies, per cookie: Calories: 67; Total Fat: 2 g (Sat. Fat: 0.1 g); Cholesterol: 0 mg; Carbohydrate: 11.8 g; Fiber: 0.7 g; Protein: 0.8 g.

> *Use a food processor to grind the oats. I use "quick oats" and process them until the consistency is close to a coarse flour.*

> *If you use cane juice sugar, the cookies will be darker and less crispy, but will still taste great. The unrefined sugar I use is similar to white sugar in appearance, but with larger granules and golden in color.*

> *Try adding 2-3 tbsp of toasted chopped nuts to the batter, such as pecans or walnuts.*

Ooey-Gooey Caramel Chip Bars

CARAMEL CENTER:

2 cups	vanilla soy milk
½ cup	unrefined sugar
	pinch sea salt
2-3 tsp	water
2 tsp	arrowroot powder
1 tsp	pure vanilla extract

GRAHAM CRACKER BOTTOM:

1 cup	graham cracker crumbs (see sidebar)
½ cup	quick oats
	few pinches sea salt
1½ tbsp	honey option (for notes on honey options, see p. 29)
1 tbsp	pure maple syrup
1½ tbsp	canola oil

TOPPING:

2 tbsp	unsweetened shredded coconut
3-4 tbsp	non-dairy chocolate chips

For caramel center: in a saucepan over medium-high heat, combine soy milk, sugar, and salt. Bring to a boil, then reduce heat to medium-low and simmer, stirring occasionally, for 30-40 minutes. Mixture should be thick and caramelized, and reduced to about 1 cup. Mix the water with the arrowroot, stirring to a smooth consistency. Slowly stir arrowroot mixture into saucepan, mixing well, and bring back to a low boil. Remove from heat and stir in vanilla. Preheat oven to 350°F. In a bowl, combine ingredients for graham cracker bottom, working mixture with your fingers until well combined. Press mixture evenly into an 8"x8" pan lined with parchment paper, or lightly oiled (see sidebar). Pour caramel evenly on crust, sprinkle on shredded coconut and chocolate chips, and bake for 18-21 minutes, until coconut is golden and caramel is bubbling in spots. Let cool, and cut into squares.

Makes 12-16 squares.

♥ For 16 squares, per square: Calories: 116; Total Fat: 4.2 g (Sat. Fat: 1.4 g); Cholesterol: 0 mg; Carbohydrate: 17.9 g; Fiber: 1.2 g; Protein: 2 g.

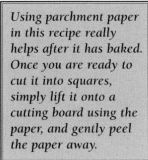

I use low-fat graham crackers and grind them in a food processor, to make my own crumbs.

◆

Using parchment paper in this recipe really helps after it has baked. Once you are ready to cut it into squares, simply lift it onto a cutting board using the paper, and gently peel the paper away.

Swallow-It-All Banana Balls

¼ cup	apple, minced
1 tsp + 1 tsp lemon juice	
½ cup	ripe banana, mashed
½ cup	dates, chopped
2 tbsp	almond butter or other natural nut butter
½-¾ cup	crushed corn flakes (see sidebar)
½ cup	ground oats (see sidebar)
3 tbsp	unsweetened shredded coconut
2 tbsp	flaxmeal
2-3 tbsp	carob powder and/or unsweetened shredded coconut (optional, to finish cookies; can use all carob or all coconut, or omit altogether)

In a bowl, toss apple with 1 tsp lemon juice, and in another bowl, combine banana with the other 1 tsp lemon juice and mix well. In a food processor or blender, combine dates, banana, and almond butter and purée until mixture starts to liquefy. In a mixing bowl, combine purée with remaining ingredients (except the optional carob powder/shredded coconut), mixing well. Take spoonfuls of mixture and form into golf-sized balls, rolling them gently between your palms. Roll each ball in carob powder or shredded coconut. Refrigerate them until chilled, or enjoy right away.
Makes 10-12 banana balls.

♥ For 12 banana balls (using carob powder), per ball: Calories: 95; Total Fat: 3.1 g (Sat. Fat: 1 g); Cholesterol: 0 mg; Carbohydrate: 14.9 g; Fiber: 2.6 g; Protein: 1.7 g.

These no-bake cookies will be a hit with your kids - and with you, as they're loaded with nutritious grains, fruits, and nuts (and no added sugar). They also freeze well for a quick snack on the run!

The more crushed corn flakes you use, the firmer the cookies will be. I use just over ½ cup, since I like these cookies moist. They will firm up once rolled and cooled, because the crushed corn flakes, oats, and flaxmeal will absorb some of the moisture.

Use a food processor to grind the oats. I use "quick oats" and process them until the consistency is close to a coarse flour.

Apple Cherry Crisp

FRUIT MIXTURE:

3 tbsp	pure maple syrup
2 tsp	arrowroot powder
2 cups	apples, cored, peeled, and chopped
2 tsp	lemon juice (preferably fresh)
2 cups	fresh cherries, stemmed and pitted (see sidebar)
1 tsp	pure vanilla extract
¼ tsp	cinnamon
¼ tsp	fresh nutmeg, grated
	pinch sea salt

CRISP TOPPING:

1-1¼ cup	quick oats (see sidebar)
1 tbsp	unrefined sugar
½-¾ tsp	cinnamon
	few good pinches sea salt
2 tbsp	pure maple syrup
1 tbsp	canola oil

Preheat oven to 350°F. For fruit mixture, mix maple syrup and arrowroot until smooth. In a large bowl, toss apples with lemon juice, then add maple syrup mixture and remaining fruit mixture ingredients, and mix well. Transfer mixture to a lightly oiled 8"x8" baking dish. For the topping, in another bowl, combine oats, sugar, cinnamon, and salt. Mix well, then add maple syrup and canola oil. Work mixture with your hands, then sprinkle evenly over the fruit, lightly pressing down. Bake for 38-43 minutes until bubbling around the edges and lightly browned. Remove and cool a little before serving.

Serves 4-5.

♥ For 5 servings, per serving: Calories: 237; Total Fat: 4.5 g (Sat. Fat: 0.5 g); Cholesterol: 0 mg; Carbohydrate: 45.1 g; Fiber: 4.4 g; Protein: 3.9 g.

Substitution Note: Other fresh berries or fruits, or frozen cherries, can be used when cherries aren't in season. If using frozen, the baking time will extend to 50-55 minutes.

I prefer a thin layer of topping, so I use just 1 cup of oats. For a topping that's a little thicker, use the extra ¼ cup.

If serving warm, pair this crisp with non-dairy vanilla ice-cream or "Almond Whipped Cream" (p. 172).

Baked Lime (or Lemon) "Cream" Pie

PIE CRUST (OR USE A PREPARED CRUST):

1½ cups	graham cracker crumbs (see sidebar)
3½-4 tbsp	honey option (for notes on honey options, see p. 29)
1½-2 tbsp	canola oil
	few good pinches sea salt

FILLING:

¼ cup	cashews or blanched almonds
1	300-g pkg soft tofu (roughly 1¼ cups), patted dry
½ cup	unrefined sugar
2 tbsp	pure maple syrup
¼ cup	fresh lime or lemon juice
¼ cup	unbleached all-purpose flour
2 tsp	pure vanilla extract
	pinch sea salt
1 tsp	lime or lemon zest

TOPPING:

1½-2½ cups	prepared vanilla pudding (see sidebar)

You can make one or two pies with this recipe, depending on the size of your pie plate. The vanilla pudding deepens the flavors of this pie, but you can make the pie without it. If you do, I suggest making just one large pie, so the filling will be generous!

I use low-fat graham crackers and grind them in a food processor to make my own crumbs.

IF MAKING PIE CRUST:

Preheat oven to 350°F. In a bowl, combine ingredients and mix well, using your fingers to reach a crumbly texture that sticks together somewhat when pressed. Place in a large pie pan (or two smaller ones), pressing down mixture, and bake for 6-8 minutes, until lightly browned. Remove from oven and let cool.

FOR THE FILLING:

Preheat oven to 350°F. In a food processor, process cashews or blanched almonds until very fine, almost powdery. Add tofu and purée until smooth, scraping down the sides of the processor a few times. Add remaining ingredients except lime/lemon zest and continue to blend until very smooth. Stir in the lime or lemon zest and pour mixture into your pie shell(s). Bake for 24-25 minutes for one larger pie, or 18-19 minutes for two smaller pies. Remove from oven and let cool completely (it will thicken more once cool). If using vanilla pudding topping, generously and gently spread pudding over top of pie(s) to preferred thickness. Refrigerate before serving, then slice into pieces and serve.

♥ For 8 slices, per slice: Calories: 331; Total Fat: 9.1 g (Sat. Fat: 1.6 g); Cholesterol: 0 mg; Carbohydrate: 55.4 g; Fiber: 2.2 g; Protein: 7.1 g.

For the topping, Mori-Nu pudding mate mix is superb. Use the dry vanilla pudding mix, and blend with Mori-Nu extra-firm lite silken tofu and some soy milk. I use one mix for one larger pie (yields 1½ cups pudding), and between 1 and 2 mixes for two smaller pies. If you can't find Mori-Nu pudding mix, use another vanilla pudding, or prepare without pudding and spoon dollops of "Almond Whipped Cream" (p. 172) over individual servings.

Blueberry-Orange Crisp Cake

½ cup	unbleached all-purpose flour
1½ tsp	baking powder
½ tsp	baking soda
1¼ cup	ground oats (see sidebar)
¾ cup	unrefined sugar
	couple pinches cinnamon
	few pinches sea salt
1 cup	vanilla or plain soy milk
2 tsp	pure vanilla extract
1-1½ tsp	orange or lemon zest
1½ cups	fresh or frozen blueberries (see sidebar)
2 tbsp	canola oil
1½-2 tbsp	unrefined sugar (for topping)

Preheat oven to 350°F. Sift together flour, baking powder, and baking soda, then stir in remaining dry ingredients except the 1½-2 tbsp sugar for topping, and mix well. Stir in soy milk, vanilla extract, and orange zest. As mixture starts to come together, add blueberries and canola oil, mixing until just well combined. (If using frozen blueberries, remove from the freezer just before adding; do not thaw. Work them through the batter fairly quickly and bake right away, so blueberries retain most of their form.) Pour batter evenly into a lightly oiled 8"x12" pan, then gently tap pan on the countertop to remove any air and help even out the batter. Sprinkle the 1½-2 tbsp sugar evenly over mixture. Bake for 32-38 minutes until golden and a toothpick inserted in the center comes out clean. Remove from oven and cool in pan a little before cutting into pieces.

Makes 6-8 medium to large pieces.

♥ For 8 pieces, per piece: Calories: 221; Total Fat: 5 g (Sat. Fat: 0.4 g); Cholesterol: 0 mg; Carbohydrate: 40.3 g; Fiber: 2.6 g; Protein: 3.8 g.

Substitution Idea: Other berries can be substituted in whole, or in part, for the blueberries, including raspberries, straw-berries, and/or pitted cherries.

◆

Use a food processor to grind the oats. I use "quick oats" and process them until the consistency is close to a coarse flour.

◆

This is great served warm, especially with vanilla soy ice cream or "Almond Whipped Cream" (p. 172), but is also nice served cool. For a mid-day treat, the squares can be wrapped and packed for lunches.

Coconut "Cream" Pie

This pie is truly heavenly: a luscious and creamy filling and a delicious, comforting granola crust. It's yet another dessert that will surprise those who think rich, velvety desserts need milk, cream, or butter!

◆

Use a food processor to grind the oats. I use "quick oats" and process them until the consistency is close to a coarse flour.

◆

If you don't serve this pie immediately, you can refrigerate the filling in a separate container from the crust, and then fill the pie within a couple of hours of serving. This will help keep the crust crispy.

PIE CRUST (OR USE A PREPARED CRUST):

1¼ cup	ground oats (see sidebar)
½ cup	quick oats
3 tbsp	honey option (for notes on honey options, see p. 29)
2 tbsp	pure maple syrup
1-1½ tbsp	canola oil
	few good pinches sea salt

FILLING:

1	300-g pkg soft tofu (roughly 1¼ cups)
1 cup	low-fat coconut milk
¼ cup	unrefined sugar
2 tbsp	pure maple syrup
3 tbsp	arrowroot flour
	couple pinches sea salt
¾ cup	shredded unsweetened coconut
½ tsp	pure vanilla extract
¼-½ tsp	coconut extract

If making pie crust: preheat oven to 350°F. In a bowl, combine ingredients and mix well, using your fingers to reach a crumbly texture that sticks together somewhat when pressed. Press mixture into a 9" pie pan. Bake for 10-13 minutes until golden around the edges. Remove from oven and let cool. **For the filling:** in a food processor or blender, combine tofu, coconut milk, sugar, maple syrup, arrowroot flour, and salt, and purée until smooth. Transfer mixture to a saucepan and stir in coconut. Over medium heat, slowly bring mixture to a thick, slow boil, stirring frequently. Remove from heat, stir in vanilla and coconut extracts. Let cool, uncovered, stirring occasionally for 10 minutes. Cover pot to cool completely (will take over an hour, refrigerate to cool more quickly). Pour mixture into pie crust and refrigerate to set.

♥ For 8 slices, per slice: Calories: 281; Total Fat: 12.2 g (Sat. Fat: 6.7 g); Cholesterol: 0 mg; Carbohydrate: 37.6 g; Fiber: 3.4 g; Protein: 5.4 g.

Lusciously Light Tiramisu

CAKE:

2 cups	unbleached all-purpose flour
1 tsp	baking powder
1 tsp	baking soda
1 cup	unrefined sugar
	few pinches sea salt
¾ cup	water
½ cup	vanilla or plain soy milk
1 tbsp	seasoned rice vinegar
2 tsp	pure vanilla extract
½ tsp	almond extract
2½-3 tbsp	canola oil

"CREAM":

2	340-g pkgs silken firm tofu
1	300-g pkg dessert tofu
1	vanilla bean (see sidebar)
¾ cup	maple syrup sugar or icing sugar (see sidebar)
½ tsp	pure vanilla extract
¼ tsp	almond extract

FINISH:

¾ cup	Kahlua or another coffee liqueur (see sidebar)
¾ cup	very strong coffee, cooled (see sidebar)
½-¾ cup	non-dairy chocolate chips, puréed until crumbly

This version of tiramisu passes on the heavy cream, cheeses, and butter for lighter, healthier ingredients. The recipe for the cake alone can also be used for a simple double-layer yellow cake (great for a birthday cake!).

Using a vanilla bean is really wonderful in this recipe. Vanilla beans can be found in most grocery stores, but if you can't find them, use an extra ½-1 tsp of vanilla extract, adjusting to taste.

Maple syrup sugar is a fine, granulated sugar made from boiling maple syrup to evaporate the liquid. It works very well here, since its texture is so fine and its flavor so great. It can be found in health food stores, but if you can't find it, substitute icing sugar – adding it gradually to adjust sweetness to taste.

◆

You can use less of the Kahlua and coffee mixture if you like. I have also made this with a coffee substitute, so this is another alternative you can try if desired.

FOR THE CAKE:

Preheat oven to 350°F. In a bowl, sift together flour, baking powder, and baking soda, then mix in sugar and salt, combining well. In another bowl, combine water, soy milk, vinegar, and vanilla and almond extracts. Add wet mixture to dry ingredients and stir together. Add canola oil as it starts to come together, stirring until just combined. Pour batter into two lightly oiled cake pans, then gently tap the pans on the countertop to remove any air and to flatten out the batter more. Bake for 22-25 minutes, until lightly golden and a toothpick inserted in the center comes out clean.

FOR THE "CREAM":

In a food processor or blender, combine tofus and purée until very smooth, scraping down the bowl a couple of times. Slice vanilla bean lengthwise, and using a knife, scrape out most of the vanilla seeds. Add seeds, along with sugar and vanilla and almond extracts, and purée again until completely smooth.

TO FINISH:

Mix Kahlua and coffee together. Cut cake into thin slices (about ¼" thick), then cut slices into 2 or 3 pieces to make them easier to work with. Cover the bottom of a large bowl with a layer of cake slices. Drizzle the coffee/Kahlua mixture over layer, then top with tofu cream, about ½" deep. Sprinkle chocolate chip crumbs over cream to cover. Continue layering two or three more times, until the bowl is nearly full, and finish with a fairly thick layer of tofu cream, topped with more chocolate chips. You may not use all of the cake, but you will likely use all of the tofu cream. Keep in mind that the kahlua/coffee mixture tends to seep to the bottom of the bowl, so be more generous with the mixture at the top than at the bottom, to ensure lots of flavor at the top! Let refrigerate for a couple of hours or overnight, then serve in individual bowls. *Serves 6-8.*

♥ For 8 servings, per serving: Calories: 389; Total Fat: 8.7 g (Sat. Fat: 0.8 g); Cholesterol: 0 mg; Carbohydrate: 67 g; Fiber: 1.2 g; Protein: 10.5 g.

Triple Layer Chocolate "Cream" Cake

CAKE:

2 cups	unbleached all-purpose flour
½ cup	cocoa powder
2 tsp	baking soda
1½ cups	unrefined sugar
	few pinches sea salt
1¾ cups	water
2 tbsp	seasoned rice vinegar
1 tsp	pure vanilla extract
1 tsp	mocha extract (or more vanilla)
¼ cup	canola oil

ICING:

2	349-g pkgs silken firm or silken extra-firm tofu (or combination), patted dry
¼ cup	pure maple syrup
2 tsp	pure vanilla extract
1¾ cups	(generous) non-dairy chocolate chips (see sidebar)

I bake this cake in either 3 round cake pans, or in 1 rimmed cookie sheet (once baked, you can slice the cake into 3 rectangular pieces for a 3-layer cake).

◆

You can also make cupcakes with this cake batter! Pour batter into cupcake liners in a muffin pan (will make 12-14 cupcakes). Bake for 24-28 minutes, until a toothpick inserted in the center comes out clean. Once cool, spread icing over each cupcake. Note that you will have a lot of icing left over, enough for another batch of cupcakes, if you wish!

FOR THE CAKE:

Preheat oven to 350°F. In a bowl, sift together flour, cocoa powder, and baking soda, then add in sugar and salt. Mix well. Stir in water, vinegar, and vanilla extract. Add in canola oil as the mixture starts to come together, and stir until just well combined. Pour into 3 round or square cake pans, or into a lightly oiled, 12"x19" rimmed cooking sheet. Gently tap pan(s) on countertop to remove any air and to even out batter more. Bake for 17-20 minutes, until a toothpick inserted in the center comes out clean. Remove from oven and let cool on cooling rack. If using cooking sheet, once the cake is cool, cut into 3 equal rectangular pieces, along the longest edge of cake.

FOR THE ICING:

In a food processor, combine tofu with maple syrup and vanilla extract and purée until very smooth, scraping down the bowl a couple of times. In a saucepan over boiling water, melt chocolate chips (for tips on melting chocolate, see p. 36), then while puréeing tofu mixture, pour in melted chocolate. Purée until very smooth and consistent, again scraping down the bowl a couple of times. Transfer to a container to refrigerate until completely cool, at least several hours (the icing will thicken a lot once cooled). Spread the icing on the cake layers, then refrigerate the cake for at least a couple of hours, to set. (I like to use all of the icing on the cake, since once the cake chills, it firms up with the icing.)

♥ For 12 slices, per slice: Calories: 473; Total Fat: 15.9 g (Sat. Fat: 6.8 g); Cholesterol: 0 mg; Carbohydrate: 72.8 g; Fiber: 4.6 g; Protein: 9.5 g.

The tofu icing is creamy and delicious, but not overly sweet. I like to splurge when making it and use very good chocolate, such as callebaut. It's a little more expensive and usually requires a trip to a specialty or health food store, but its texture is so smooth and pure, it's truly awesome in this icing!

Why Deny? Ice-Cream Pie

1 batch	"Hot Fudge Sauce," (p. 176)

PIE CRUST (OR USE A PREPARED CRUST):

1½ cups	graham cracker crumbs (see sidebar)
3½-4 tbsp	honey option (for notes on honey options, see p. 29)
1½-2 tbsp	canola oil
	few good pinches sea salt
4-5 cups	commercial soy ice cream, any flavor (see sidebar)

Prepare hot fudge sauce and let cool completely (put in refrigerator if needed).

IF YOU ARE MAKING THE PIE CRUST:

Preheat oven to 350°F. In a bowl, combine ingredients and mix well, using your fingers to reach a crumbly texture that sticks together somewhat when pressed. Press into a large pie pan, and bake for 6-8 minutes, until lightly browned. Remove from oven and let cool. Allow ice cream to soften a little at room temperature or in the refrigerator. Spoon softened ice cream into the pie crust. Place in the freezer until ice cream has hardened again. Remove and top the pie with the fudge sauce, spreading evenly over the top (you should be able to use most of the sauce). Place back in the freezer to firm up again (the hot fudge sauce will not be completely firm), and serve.

♥ For 8 slices (using Mint Marble Fudge "Soy Delicious" ice cream), per slice: Calories: 376; Total Fat: 10.2 g (Sat. Fat: 1.3 g); Cholesterol: 0 mg; Carbohydrate: 66.1 g; Fiber: 3 g; Protein: 5 g.

My favorite soy ice creams are the organic "Soy Delicious" varieties, including Chocolate Velvet and Creamy Vanilla. Jazz them up even more and mix in your favorite "chunky" ingredients, such as non-dairy chocolate chips, or toasted nuts.

I use low-fat graham crackers and grind them in a food processor to make my own crumbs.

Try topping slices with a simple fruit sauce; it gives a tangy contrast to the pie, and is easy to make. In a blender, purée frozen berries, such as strawberries, with a little apple or orange juice and a little water until smooth but still a little thick. Adjust the sweetness with a little maple syrup. You can also add a touch of pure vanilla extract. Keep the sauce a little thick, since it will thin out as it thaws.

Index

Index

Index

Index

Index

Index

Index